"In a culture that fears aging and perpetuates ideals of youthfulness over valuing the elderly, *The Joy Document* offers wisdom that honors the process of growing older. I admire Jennifer McGaha's insight on embracing life's simple moments with gratitude and joy. Despite facing loss and navigating through challenging times like a global crisis, there's still opportunity to find joy in the here and now."

Rainie Howard, author of *The Love Habit*
and host of *The Rainie Howard Show*

"With her beautiful storytelling, Jennifer McGaha inspires us to join her in creating a light-filled life. Through a commitment to curiosity, to mindful noticing, to gratitude, to joyful celebration, she epitomizes what it means to be a radiant rebel!"

Karen Walrond, author of *Radiant Rebellion*
and *The Lightmaker's Manifesto*

"Jennifer McGaha is that trail partner who calls you back when you've marched ahead, to show you a lady slipper hidden under a fern. Her joys will open your eyes to your own."

Heather Newton, author of *The Puppeteer's Daughters*

THE JOY
DOCUMENT

THE JOY DOCUMENT

Creating a Midlife of Surprise and Delight

Jennifer McGaha

Broadleaf Books

Minneapolis

THE JOY DOCUMENT
Creating a Midlife of Surprise and Delight

29 28 27 26 25 24   1 2 3 4 5 6 7 8 9

Library of Congress Cataloging-in-Publication Data
Names: McGaha, Jennifer, author.
Title: The joy document : creating a midlife of surprise and delight /
   Jennifer McGaha.
Other titles: Creating a midlife of surprise and delight
Description: Minneapolis : Broadleaf Books, [2024]
Identifiers: LCCN 2023058906 (print) | LCCN 2023058907 (ebook) | ISBN
   9798889830726 (hardcover) | ISBN 9798889830733 (ebook)
Subjects: LCSH: Joy.
Classification: LCC BJ1481 .M45 2024 (print) | LCC BJ1481 (ebook) | DDC
   152.4/2--dc23/eng/20240318
LC record available at https://lccn.loc.gov/2023058906
LC ebook record available at https://lccn.loc.gov/2023058907

Cover image: © 2023 Getty Images; Inclusion and diversity infographic vector set, people vector logo for website/2090435689 by iam2mai
Cover design: Faceout Studios

Print ISBN: 979-8-8898-3072-6
eBook ISBN: 979-8-8898-3073-3

Printed in China.

*In loving memory of April Lewis Lindsay,
my fellow troublemaker and joy seeker for
over two decades.*

CONTENTS

INTRODUCTION

In 1974, in a Pentecostal church in Canton, North Carolina, the choir sang "How Great Thou Art" as men in suits, women in dresses and heels, and kids, hair slicked back or fastened in barrettes, poured through the heavy wooden doors. Like my grandfather, most of these people worked at Champion, the local paper mill. They dressed up only for church services, funerals, and weddings, and even to a seven-year-old, they looked strangely out of place in their Sunday best.

My brother, grandparents, and I settled onto a hard pew near the back of the church, the choir took their seats, the congregation fell silent, and the preacher made his way to the podium. Opening his Bible, he ran his hand through his shiny black hair, then cleared his throat and began. His cheeks flushed, and his voice grew louder and faster, more insistent as he preached. He raised one hand, looked to the heavens, then pointed a trembling finger in our direction.

I ducked down, tried to make myself smaller, a speck of dust on the pew. In my lap, my interlocked hands formed a church. My thumbs were the church doors, my forefingers the steeple. Inside, imaginary people danced. This was the way I fell asleep most nights, my hands casting church shadows on my bedroom walls. I was an anxious child, and these images soothed me somehow. The memory of them soothes me still, though I struggle to articulate how or why. The church was a source of joy for me. The church was a source of terror for me. Those two truths existed side by side, and perhaps creating my own miniature churches was my first attempt at reconciling those truths, at capturing what I could hold and releasing the rest.

When I finally got the courage to look up again, the preacher was still screaming, and a woman sitting on the pew in front of us moaned and swayed. She made her way to her feet, raised her hands in the air, and, hollering incoherently, darted into the aisle. When she fell to her knees, her long dress falling around her like a Christmas tree skirt, I covered my ears and ducked down, tucking my head between my legs as my mother had instructed me to do whenever I felt faint (which was surprisingly often for a child my age).

Though my grandparents were religious in their own way, they weren't churchgoing people, and during the many, many Sundays I spent with them, this was one of the few times we went to church together. Most Sundays, my brother and I attended services at the staid Presbyterian church in Brevard, where we lived, about forty miles away. There, people spoke in hushed tones, and the preacher was more of a kindly professor of sorts. The rhetoric was not gentle, but the delivery was. Still, nothing about this service seemed to surprise anyone but me. My grandparents and brother sat calmly, quietly, but soon everyone around us was on their feet, arms flailing, eyes closed, faces turned heavenward, their wailing one wave—rising, rising, rising.

In Sunday school at my parents' church, I had learned about the second coming, when the sky would open and Christ would return in a brilliant, holy flash, just before he sent all the murderers and whoremongers and pregnant women directly through the earth to writhe in eternal agony. Then, the righteous dead would be resurrected, and those of us still living, the forgiven, the chosen, would go directly to heaven to sit at the right hand of God. At the time, this had sounded like a fate worse than perpetually burning. I could not imagine anything more torturous, more lonely, more *boring* than sitting next to God all day long for all eternity. Hell sounded infinitely more interesting, but also scary and quite possibly painful, so I lived in almost constant fear of the rapture. As the whole church swayed and rocked and moaned, I began to wonder whether this could be the end of times. Or was this perhaps something even *worse*?

At a church just down the road, people regularly handled rattlesnakes, and the police sometimes hauled the snake handlers away to jail. I knew this because my grandfather often regaled us with these stories at the dinner table.

"Hush, Hubert," my grandmother would say. "You're scaring Jennifer."

But trying not to scare me was a waste of energy. Like the Japanese beetles that devoured my grandparents' grapevines and the stench of the paper mill on stifling summer days, my anxiety was inevitable, something we all eventually learned to work around. Now, though no one had specifically mentioned the rapture or handling rattlesnakes, this felt like the sort of situation where one or both of those things might come to pass. Each felt equally terrifying in its own way.

As the church thundered and shook, the stained-glass windows rattling, the wooden cross at the front of the church vibrating, fat tears rolled down my cheeks and fell onto my new red dress. I wiped my face with my sweater sleeve, and that's when my grandmother noticed that I was afraid. She gathered me onto her lap, where I lay with one ear pressed against her leg while she covered my other ear with her hand.

For a moment, the noises became a distant hum, a gentle vibration, but soon my grandmother's slender thighs began to twitch, then roll, then heave up and down. My body rocked with her, a fishing bobber on the Pigeon River, tossing with the foamy current until I finally realized she was laughing, not *at me*, exactly, but, if I had to guess, at the unexpectedness of it all, at the spectacle of the child curled into fetal position while people thrashed in ecstasy in the aisles. Her amusement, though, was oddly reassuring. I still did not know what we were witnessing, but I knew then that if she was laughing, we would likely survive it, that this wasn't the rapture after all. In that instant, I was, for once in my life, perfectly at ease. Everyone and everything else faded away—the shrieking and moaning and thrashing, the threats of eternal damnation, the threats of eternal salvation. Only my grandmother and I remained as she leaned in close to my ear.

"It's okay," she whispered. "It's okay. They're just prayin'."

Over fifty years later, I can still feel the thin fabric of her polyester skirt against my cheek, her warm breath tickling my ear, the gentle weight of her arm on my hip bone. In so many ways, I have been there ever since, huddled on a hard pew in an evangelical church in Haywood County, wrapped in my grandmother's arms, my faith borne more of whom I loved and where I was loved than any particular doctrine, the hallelujahs, the amens, and the exultations so deeply embedded in my *Appalachianness* that I often struggle to discern the difference. Perhaps there is no difference, only the simple truth that all I know of the divine, of giving thanks, of holding tightly to those you love, and of believing in something larger than yourself, even when you don't know exactly what that is, I have learned from this place and these people.

Now, over a decade after my grandmother's death, her wisdom remains a guiding force in my life. Once, when she was in her late eighties and I was in my forties, roughly the same age she was when I was born, I asked her what her favorite age so far had been.

"Fifty-five," she said.

I cannot recall what prompted the discussion, but at the time I believed she responded as she did to be generous, to give me something to look forward to. Then, when I was in my fifties, I began to consider that perhaps she had said it earnestly, that she sincerely believed there was something magical about this stage of life, some deeper way of being that was knowable only from this vantage point. It was also a time in my life when more and more of my friends and family were sick or dying, when, like a grassy field in the aftermath of a storm, the colors of my life were particularly intense, as if I were seeing everything for the first time, the past and the present. I was firmly engrossed in the business of living while keenly aware, for perhaps the first time, of how fragile it all was. I wanted to mark this year in some way, to take note, and somewhere along the way, I began to realize I was chronicling my experiences, yes, but also reseeing and reshaping my perceptions as I wrote about them.

I realize that, more often than not, my life has offered examples of what *not* to do versus what *to* do (ask anyone who knows me well—my family, my closest friends), so I hesitate to be too instructive here, to assert that I now know the secret to embracing this stage of life. Still, the essays here are my attempts at capturing the joyful experiences that were uniquely mine during this year yet somehow, hopefully, point to something more universal, a way of approaching midlife that honors and cultivates surprise and delight.

Each day during my fifty-fifth year, whenever I had a free moment, between teaching classes or while in my car waiting for the rain to stop or standing at the kitchen counter as my coffee slowly brewed, I jotted down my impressions of simple, everyday things that struck me as beautiful or humorous or intriguing: a particularly delectable cup of Swedish crème from a local bakery, an encounter with a stranger on a trail or at the grocery store, a mother possum carrying her young on her back, a male goat in the throes of romantic passion, a convoluted phrase in a student essay, and so on. I see now that, as I wrote about teaching, running, listening to music, traveling, and so on, I was writing about those ordinary moments that add up to a life. The process was the opposite of peeling an onion. It was the *unpeeling* of an onion, if you will. Or perhaps it was more like making a no-bake chocolate éclair cake where you layer graham crackers with a custard made of pudding and Cool Whip, then top it all off with chocolate frosting and refrigerate it overnight. When you take it out of the refrigerator the next day, everything has glopped together into something almost unrecognizable from before. Nothing has changed, yet everything has.

As I wrote, I considered what I most wanted to know. For example, how could I learn to be grateful for what I have, to be joyful in the moment even when there were so many reasons not to be—close friends and family members dying, a global pandemic, the rise of hatred and bigotry in all its forms, a rapidly escalating climate crisis, a country in which almost half its citizens pledge blind allegiance to a political party that does not work in their best interest, and on and on? How could I learn to honor the sense of loss and grief and regret and, hell, just general dismay that comes with living for over half a century without succumbing to it? And what would happen if I attempted to approach each day and each interaction with joyful intention? In other words, how might my life—how might *all* our lives—like chocolate éclair cake, grow more nuanced and richer as we grow older?

Intrigued by these questions, I kept going. The only rule I set for myself was that each essay must spring from a specific, current moment in time—no diving into the past, no relying on old Microsoft Word documents gathering metaphorical dust on my hard drive. If this book were going to be about finding joy in this moment, the essays needed to be grounded in the present. Though I struggled a bit with the definition of the fifty-fifth year (Did it begin on my fifty-fifth birthday—July 20, 2021—and end on my fifty-sixth birthday? Or did it begin on my fifty-fourth and end on my fifty-fifth?), I soon decided not to stress too much about the exact day something happened and to call it good if something happened roughly during this time. (This became, now that I think about it, one of the first lessons of this journey: cut yourself some slack whenever and however you can.)

The examination of joy is not a novel concept, and while writing this book, I spent time studying other creative works that have explored this topic, including Zadie Smith's mesmerizing essay "Joy" (from her essay collection *Feel Free*) as well as Ross Gay's *Book of Delights*. Both Gay and Smith examine joy as a complex emotion experienced only when we understand on a deep level what connects us as human beings—an awareness of our own mortality. Because we will die, because everyone we love will die, each moment is all the more precious, all the more glorious. I also read Terry Tempest Williams's *When Women Were Birds*, Aimee Nezhukumatathil's *World of Wonders*, and other books infused with a sense of both celebration and searching. Through all my readings, I was struck most profoundly with the sense that it is possible to intentionally cultivate a life full of gratitude for the here and now, a life awash with joy and optimism and even humor. After all, what else are we to do in the face of so much despair?

Writing this book has allowed me to examine my own life, to discover hidden wisdom and unexpected beauty, but it has also prompted me to reflect on this larger moment when examining how we got here as a society and where we might go from here seems of paramount importance. For me, those greater truths are revealed most clearly in small, everyday moments like the ones I've gathered here, moments that underscore the urgency of learning to live in greater harmony with the land and with one another, of working tirelessly to preserve and protect the people and places and beliefs we hold dear.

Here is what I now know: There are times in your life when joy, like a crocus poking through the hard dirt in February, will sneak up and catch you unaware. Those moments are, indeed, rare and delightful gifts. More often, though, joy is harder to come by, and you must go searching for it. Maybe there are no crocuses this February, just clusters of dead grass in the spaces where they normally bloom. Perhaps there has been too much snow or not enough snow, too much rain, or too little light, or too many neighborhood kids kicking soccer balls through the grass, or too many dogs peeing in just this spot.

Not to worry. Crocuses are one source of joy, one thing to love about early spring, but there are other things. Perhaps, if you look hard enough, you might find mayfly larvae in the creek bed by your house, or clusters of frog eggs in the dip on the mountain trail where you run, the place where rainwater gathers and mosquitoes breed wildly in the summertime. Perhaps you will come upon that teeming puddle on a cold, winter day and be amazed by the firm, translucent, jelly-like eggs, by the tiniest dark hints of frogs-to-be visible through the surface, promises of mosquito catchers to come. Imagine the joy in that, the way it might forever change how you look at puddles, how you wait and watch for spring.

Most of the joy I have found in my life has been like that joy, tadpole joy, joy-in-the-making I have discovered when I have been open to receiving it in whatever form it comes. After a year of examining it, it seems to me that joy must go hand in hand with gratitude, that being thankful for the many gifts of this life is not a luxury but a vital, radical mindset, not unlike growing your own garden or booking a plane ticket a year out or adopting a dachshund with an average lifespan of twelve to sixteen years, all these things being a resounding rejection of despondency and dejection and despair and a fervent embracing of all that is and gracious and good and true. It is also a reminder to, in the words of Peloton's Andy Speer, keep our pain at a level that is "uncomfortable but not unmanageable," to push through the hard things in search not of lemonade in the presence of lemons, not a superficial cheeriness or glass-half-fullness, but the strength that comes from finding what you love, what amazes and inspires you, and naming it.

Perhaps this book is also a way of reclaiming what has been lost to me, a way of hoping out loud, of wishing on the page, of returning once more to 1974, to that church in that mountain mill town where people spoke in tongues, which I think of now and again—more often now than before, perhaps—those voices thick with freight-train whistles and tobacco and sweat and cornbread crumbled into buttermilk and laundry drying on the line, and I hear them now anew, which is to say I hear them now finally without fear but with awe, their invocations and attestations not so much lamentations but celebrations for the many ways the day-to-day, the everyday, the mundane, and even the profane might, if we hold these things to the light *just so*, become a form of thanksgiving.

This world is our church. Our hands form a steeple. Open the doors, and here we all are—so many beautiful people.

1

THE JOY DOCUMENT

AT THE END of every academic year, after exams have been administered, grades have been submitted, and all the hoopla surrounding graduation is over, my university colleagues and I are charged with submitting our annual faculty records, a detailed accounting of all the things we have done over the course of the year to justify our continued employment. This task weighs especially heavy on contingent faculty, those of us on one-, two-, and three-year contracts, and it must be completed before we can begin summering in earnest.

You can be brief, administrators told us during the height of the pandemic. *It's just a formality.*

But everyone who knows anything about academia knows that nothing is ever brief, and nothing is ever just a formality, and if I'm brief and the person next in line for ___ (fill in the blank with a promotion or grant or course release or fellowship or other incentive here) is not brief, well, I'm screwed. By this I mean not only my chances at ___ (fill in as with the previous blank) but also more generally because everything in academia is this important, this intense, this do-it-or-die-trying.

What I am saying is that, with all this emphasis on the listable, the rankable, the categorizable, and the quantifiable, the spaces for joy at my job have not always been readily apparent. Nonetheless, in this, my fifty-fifth year, I have adopted a new mantra: *You alone are responsible for your happiness.* And it occurs to me that these pages might just be my *anti-faculty record,* if you will, my inoculation against all that devalues and delineates and degrades, which is to say, all that does not elevate the spirit. They are a record of all I have been given and all I hope to give back in return—my very own Joy Document. Naming these moments seems to me a powerful way of asserting that my life cannot be reduced to committee service and student evaluations and journal publications. Sometimes, the best stuff defies categorization, and I am learning to make note of those things too. Take, for example, the time I made Claire Saffitz's fruit-cake as a present for my dad.

At the beginning of the recipe, Claire includes a warning: if you have waited until the last minute to start this, you are, like someone who has not been thorough in their annual faculty record, thoroughly screwed. Okay, well, Claire doesn't say this exactly, but she does say that you must begin the cake at least two months before you want to eat it. Thus, like a friendship cake or sourdough bread or homemade kombucha or a homegrown jar of nocino (walnut liqueur), fruitcakes are generally best suited for the planners, the organizers, the thinkers-ahead and make-things-happeners, which is to say, *not* for people like me—the procrastinators and dilly-dalliers, the fly-by-the-seat-of-your-pantsers. Normally I am not one to stretch my limits, culinary or otherwise. To put this in college-application terms (since we are talking about higher education here), this was a *reach* recipe versus a *safety* recipe for me.

However, I wanted to make the fruitcake for my father, who has an affinity for such things, so, despite the fact that the cookbook included a note that this recipe was "challenging," I refused to be dissuaded. It turned out that making the cake wasn't especially hard, but it was a commitment. Here is how you make it: To begin, you gather nine million ingredients—nuts and assorted dried fruits and two kinds of flours and such. You soak the fruit in a combination of fresh orange juice, lemon juice, and the booze of your choice, which for me was Grand Marnier since (thanks to a young man my daughter once dated) I happened to have a spare gallon on hand. The next day, after the fruit is properly soused, you mix the batter—the fruit, two kinds of flour, spices, eggs, flavoring, orange and lemon peel, butter, sugar, molasses.

Then you bake and cool the cakes before poking holes in the tops and dousing them with—get this—*more liqueur*.

Finally (for now), you wrap them in parchment paper and again in aluminum foil and stick them in a cool, dry place safe from your pets and the occasional mouse that sneaks (chews?) through your cabin slats. (Again, I'm paraphrasing. You do you and work around whatever the challenges in your environment happen to be.) Then, once a week for the next two months, you unwrap the cakes and feed them two tablespoons of alcohol each. Of course, the tricky part here for the organizationally challenged is remembering to feed them, so you need to set many, many reminders (one day before, two hours before, one hour before, five minutes before) because if you forget, then all of the aforementioned efforts will be wasted, and you will have to wait ten more months before trying again, which is to say, you will be even more screwed than if you had missed the start date and not begun in the first place because now you're nine million ingredients and nine thousand dollars into this adventure.

Every Sunday, like a dutiful parishioner, I climbed the stairs to the spare bedroom where I kept *the girls*, as I referred to them, and before long, I had named them.

"I'm going to feed Thelma and Louise," I told my husband.

"How are Thelma and Louise?" my kids called to ask.

I spent so much time feeding them and resituating them so they weren't in direct sunlight or in front of the heat vent and so on— keeping them comfortable, in other words—that I found myself talking to them like they were pets or plants, which they sort of were. They were extended family members, little drunk outlaws crashing in our spare bedroom, and each week, when I lifted them from the Styrofoam cooler, removed the wrappings, and fed them two tablespoons of Grand Marnier each, I toasted them: *Cheers, Thelma! Cheers, Louise!*

I did this once a week for eight weeks, and you might think this would be the end of it, and if this were any ordinary fruitcake you would be, but Claire's concoction is no ordinary fruitcake.

After two months of feeding and tending, you unwrap the cakes, smother them with jam, cover every surface with a thin layer of marzipan, then top the whole shebang with frosting made from powdered sugar and egg whites.

Properly stored, the uncut, "hermetically sealed" cake could (in theory, I suppose) survive for years. Though *hermetically sealed* is not a particularly appetizing term, the entire endeavor has a hopeful energy, an uplifting, life-giving, life-affirming vibe. When I finally unwrapped the finished cakes and presented them to my astounded father, who has, frankly, always been concerned about my distractibility and incorrigibility and general lack of stick-to-itiveness, he was thrilled with his cakes, and if I do say so myself, so was I. Even though I wasn't much of a fruitcake aficionado myself, and even though most of the credit rightfully went to Claire, even I could tell this was an excellent fruitcake, as far as fruitcakes go. Thus I have added this little culinary feat to my Joy Document in celebration, yes, but also in solidarity with everyone whose worth feels contingent, conditional, dependent upon circumstances, subject to change without notice. Knowing that my department chair and dean will not be obliged to read about this on my faculty record but that you are now (hopefully) *voluntarily* reading about it here instead brings me a tremendous sense of accomplishment, and—dare I say?—joy.

So here is a slice of joy for you. And for you. And you. And you. Pass it on. And cheers to me and to you and to everyone out there still chasing joy, still celebrating those quiet achievements the sum of which is not quantifiable or categorizable but is nothing short of everything we are.

2

HANGING IN THERE (AND GOING HIGHER AND HIGHER)

ONE AUGUST AFTERNOON, on the first day of the last week of summer vacation, when the humidity was 92 percent and thunder rumbled ominously in the distance, I ran down a forest trail near my home. "Electric Avenue" played on repeat through my new headphones. I was almost at the end of my four-mile route when I saw a man walking toward me. In my overheated and somewhat disoriented state, I vaguely recognized him but couldn't place him. Stepping off the trail to let me pass, he pulled his dog close on the leash—close, but not close enough. The trail was narrow, the dog a pit bull, and though I was generally a pit fan, I didn't want to startle him (the dog, not the man).

"You can go!" I called, scanning the ground for copperheads before likewise leaping off the trail.

But the man stayed put.

"Jennifer? It's Jennifer, right?"

When he spoke, I realized we had greeted each other briefly another time, and he had reminded me then that we had gone to high school together. Now I couldn't remember his name or whether in fact he had even told me (or, rather, *re*told me).

"Yes," I said.

I hoped I wasn't yelling. I was having a hard time regulating the volume on my headphones. One tap on the right increased it. One tap on the left decreased it. Tapping and holding turned noise canceling on or off. Another tap somewhere amped up the bass, another one answered my phone, and another one ignored calls. It was difficult to remember it all. In any case, I hoped I didn't sound overly friendly because I didn't want to stop to chitchat. I was just a few hundred yards from my car, which I now very much wanted to reach. Plus, I had a fear of stopping during a run. I worried that if I stopped, I would never start again. I'm not sure when I began telling myself this, but perhaps I learned from my grandfather. Throughout my childhood, he preached the value of movement. To his way of thinking, and now mine, too, all one needed to do to stay alive was to keep moving, keep putting one foot in front of the other, one day after another, as long as you lived. How hard was that?

I was at this moment, by any objective or subjective standard, disgusting. My shirt and shorts were soaked with sweat. My hat slid and slipped and slithered around on my head. Bugs stuck to my legs. Blood ran down one arm where I had brushed against stinging nettle. I was, in other words, not at my best for reuniting with high school friends, even friends I did not remember, so I hurried past, and as I did, the guy called to me once again.

"You're really hanging in there!"

He said it kindly, enthusiastically, even, and truth be told, this was not uncommon. Often other runners and hikers and cyclists, usually men around my age or older, stopped to offer affirmations. Once, when I was out running with my hound, Homer, a cyclist stopped to ask how far we were going.

"I don't know," I said. "I'll see how far he drags me."

I kept running, but the biker was not discouraged. When I arrived back at the parking lot, he was taking a water break in the midst of his twenty-miler.

"So how far did you go?" he asked.

"I don't know."

But his friendliness was relentless. All smiles, he waited, so finally, I pulled out my phone and checked the mileage on my fitness app.

"About five," I said.

"That's terrific! That's just great!" I had watched a lot of *Ted Lasso* during the pandemic, so I imagined he said it in the way a soccer coach might, but I didn't really know since I had never actually played a sport—unless you counted cheerleading, which I sometimes did since it was all I had. "We're the best. We're the best. We're the B-E-S-T best," I had shouted in second-grade cheerleading practice.

"Jennifer, do not stick out your hip so far when you do that," my coach had said.

It was the first and last piece of coaching advice I received until I turned fifty, but since then everyone had been chock-full of fitness tips. Perhaps now the fact that I was still upright and mobile, that I was, as my high school/trail buddy put it, *hanging in there*, seemed noteworthy. Of course, *hanging in there* was not what I was going for, neither in that moment nor in life. *Hanging in there* evoked hanging by a thread or hanging on for dear life. I realized this was a glass-half-empty interpretation and that it could just as easily have meant that I was undeterred, unfazed, undaunted . . . but by what, exactly? Age? Humidity? The coming end of summer and these carefree afternoon trail runs?

I wanted my solitary presence in the woods to be like the presence of every other runner and biker here: unremarkable. Business as usual. Yet it appeared I had reached the moment in life where my continued existence was worthy of comment, like when the local radio station played an artist in his eighties and prefaced the introduction with, "He's still with us and still performing." His presence on the planet was, in other words, extraordinary. Just by existing, he was pushing boundaries, defying odds, blowing past stereotypes. He was, in other words, hanging in there.

But that was the thing about reaching this stage of life. So many people I knew were hangers-on and hanging-on-ers, and now it seemed I was one of them. So, I might as well go ahead and say it, maybe even savor it, so I thanked the former classmate I did not remember, cranked up "Electric Avenue" with one, two, three taps to my right headphone, and continued running, taking it higher and higher and higher. By the time I arrived in the parking lot, I realized I had been offered not so much an insult as a blessing, perhaps even a benediction: *May the blessing of the forest remain with you always. May you keep hanging in there all the days of your life.*

3

CARTWHEELS ON A GRAVEL ROAD

IN 1998, WHEN Lucinda Williams released her fifth album, *Car Wheels on a Gravel Road*, I heard the title track as "*Cartwheels* on a Gravel Road." Hearing it so and singing it thusly brought me much joy. As a kid, I loved doing cartwheels on thick rubber mats in gymnastics class, through my parents' living room, across the grassy field outside school . . . you get the picture—and this cartwheel cavorting did not end there.

Once, when I was in my thirties, much to the embarrassment of my three children (ranging in age from eight to thirteen, the peak years of *death by embarrassment*), I found myself spinning down a grassy knoll at Bok Tower and Gardens in Lake Wales, Florida. I had not known whether I still could do the move, whether the muscle memory required was like bike riding and would come rushing back or whether cartwheel know-how was the purview only of children and professional gymnasts, but it turned out that something of the young me prevailed. I twirled head over heels, head over heels, orchids and flowering shrubs and gigantic ferns racing past, then flashes of sunlight through the treetops, until, mercifully, I landed upright once again on the soft, perfectly manicured grass. I could do it. I had done it. Despite themselves, my children cheered.

That settled, I waited another twenty-five years before trying it again, this time on the gravel drive leading to our house. By now, I was at the age where attempting such a move meant risking more scrutiny than one might intend. Whereas at thirty-something cartwheeling down the driveway might have conveyed spontaneity, and at forty-something eccentricity, I worried it now might convey the onset of some type of condition, pre-*something*, early-onset *something*. So, I waited until I was home alone to don loose jeans and a somewhat loose but not too loose T-shirt. That way, if I failed in my attempt, my husband would not return home to find me sprawled on my back in the driveway, my body bruised and bloody, my disarrayed clothing damning evidence of my declining mental state. Then I stood on the most level spot I could find and gathered my courage.

Even though I had recently passed my bone-density screening exam with flying colors, if this went awry, there was more to lose than when I had last attempted this stunt. I now had creaky knees and tendonitis in my ankles and one particularly troublesome shoulder, the result of a biking accident a few years back. Perhaps I should have worn a helmet or at least a brace, but it was too late. I was here, committed, *all in*, and if I lost my courage doing a cartwheel, it would be all over for good, so I figured it was best not to overthink it.

I took a deep breath and threw up one leg, toes pointed, because that's how I had first seen someone do it back in 1970-something, and just like that, it *was* 1970-something, and I was nine years old, sporting short-shorts and tube socks and pigtails, wildly infatuated with both Shaun Cassidy (that Adam's apple!) and Leif Garrett (that bare chest!), who watched over me at night from the posters plastered on my bedroom wall. When I finally landed on my feet, "Cartwheels on a Gravel Road" dancing through my mind, my bravery and flexibility and still-with-it-ness etched in rock prints on my palms, I was more certain than ever that, no matter what Google or Spotify or even my husband said when I made him watch me do my groovy move over and over again that evening, the song was about both cartwheels and car wheels, about dogs and shacks and low voices, about dirt roads and getting lost and grieving, sure, but also about beginning again once again and again and again and always.

4

TWINKLY TAXI

WE WERE SCREECHING along a winding road in a taxi in another country—I won't say which one because it's a small one—while our taxi driver conducted business on his cell phone.

"Twinkly Taxi!" he announced whenever the phone rang.

Then he chatted with potential customers, most of whom were repeat customers, though God knows why. Perhaps it was because he was a fast driver and punctual. I will say that for him. When the customer asked about the dogs he raised, the driver, whose energy was not just manic but a thousand times that, turned all soft and told him that the dogs were just wonderful, just darling, and then he switched to all business again, rummaging around the front seat until he found his clipboard, flipping through a handwritten list of names and pickup times and locations. If he could fit the caller into his schedule, he added the name to the list, one hand on the clipboard, the other furiously scribbling as he steered with his knees.

The narrow road was lined with thick trees and miles-long fences, and when we met another car, we swerved toward the fences, and the trees blurred into a green screen. I was in the back middle seat, my brother on one side, my daughter on the other, my brother-in-law in front. The ride to the train station—our final destination—was only about fifteen minutes, but when I later tried to recall whether we had been in the car for an hour or for five minutes, I realized I had had no sense of time. None of it seemed real. Every time we survived a phone call and appointment booking, I was giddy with relief. Years before, I had read about a woman who talked down a serial killer simply by keeping him talking, which was perhaps what I was trying to do as, in between phone calls, I asked our driver: "How many pups do you have? What are their names? Have you found homes for all of them? Are they good with your kids?" It worked for a few blessed seconds.

"Great! They are G-R-E-A-T!" he said. "I mean, they're attack dogs, and they're trained to kill, but they're great with my kids. Just GREAT."

And then the phone rang again.

"Twinkly Taxi!"

Then, just as he was writing down the customer's contact information on his clipboard, the steering wheel nestled comfortably between his knees, we rounded a curve, and a car going almost as fast in the opposite lane pulled around a bike and into our lane. For one second, one hour, one year, we careened directly toward the oncoming car.

Perhaps we should have yelled *Stop!* Or *Look out!* Or *Help!* Something. But none of us said a word. Behind the driver, my brother did not have a clear view of what was happening, but the rest of us later confirmed that in that moment we all believed we were going to crash head-on. And everything we might have said or should have said— *Stop right here and let us out immediately*—was swallowed up in the certainty that there was nothing we could say, that saying something might in fact make this worse, which was not a conscious thought any of us had but rather a gut reaction.

Later that summer, I would be out hiking and come across a woman and her pit bull, and as I passed, the dog would make the oddest sound, a whinny-cry like I had never heard before, and I would know for certain, without being told, that this was the kill sound, the if-you-let-go-of-me-I-will-most-certainly-attack sound, and I would remember the Twinkly Taxi driver, all cheerful and bebop-y with his dirty blond, shoulder-length hair, his seventies, British-band-boy look, and that leg jiggling up and down, down and up as he swerved around curves, and I would know that in that moment when we were heading directly toward the other car, the only thing that saved us was that in the front seat beside him, my brother-in-law reached up and touched or maybe grabbed the steering wheel with one hand, and that motion somehow broke through the driver's frenzy just long enough for him to place one hand back on the wheel and guide us through the narrow opening between the green screen and the oncoming car. When we came out on the other side, the bike-passing car back in its lane, us upright in ours, I could not tell who was more crazed, him or me, so I leaned forward in my seat and asked:

"What do you feed your dogs? Is it hard to house train them all? Do you ever see the pups after they're gone?"

As if these questions alone could tether us to the pavement, as if I could will us safely to the train station, which perhaps I did, because despite everything, we screeched to a stop there, not only intact but—who would have thought it?—a few minutes early. We thanked the driver and retrieved our bags from the trunk, and as he pulled away, we doubled over laughing in relief and gratitude, which in that moment seemed to be the very same things and maybe always are.

5

STORYTELLING

ONE JULY DAY, during a pause in a days-long stretch of relentless rain, I ran into the grocery store for some essentials, by which I mean eight cartons of Ben and Jerry's. (In my defense, they were on a good sale.) When I came back out a few minutes later, I smelled it before I saw it—that musky scent like heat coming off a wet dog. Rain—again.

"Oh, no," I said.

I meant to say it to myself, but I must have said it aloud because a somewhat-older-than-me man, who was waiting under the awning with his cart full of groceries as I was, turned and nodded.

"Do you see that blue Tahoe right there?" he asked, pointing through the gray mist to the car closest to the store. I nodded. "I've got an umbrella and a rain jacket in that thing."

Then he cracked up, so I cracked up too. I wore only shorts and a T-shirt, and they both were still damp from my morning run. Still, I was in no mood to get drenched yet again.

"I thought it was over too," I said. "My phone said it was over."

I said it indignantly, as if I had been personally betrayed by the weather app, and we both laughed at that too. As thick sheets pummeled the parking lot, I thought, not for the first time this week, that this was not how I had envisioned spending my summer break. I had imagined long walks in the woods, lying on the dock by a lake, attending outdoor concerts, picking strawberries and blueberries and blackberries, sipping a seasonal sour ale while watching the sunset at a local brewery.

Instead, this persistent, insistent cold rain had left our cabin damp and my spirits even damper. Everything in our house was saturated.

My wall calendar furled and the writing was splotched, so I had no idea where I was supposed to be when. My sea salt grinder had clogged. My spices had fused to their jars. Bags of sugar and flour had molded. The lifespan of a banana left on the kitchen counter had been reduced from one day to one hour, and our bath towels were so perpetually damp that after my shower, I shook off like one of the four dogs trapped inside with us twenty-four hours a day. In the midst of all of this, I had been trying to write about joy, which was, quite frankly, becoming increasingly difficult under the circumstances.

The man and I stared silently, forlornly, into the parking lot. Finally, he spoke.

"I'm from here."

For a moment, I couldn't figure out why he had said this, but then I recognized this as shorthand for *I should have known better.* Locals here know that rain in the summer is as plentiful as mountain bikers and breweries, that it is bound to come up out of nowhere and last anywhere from five seconds to five days, that you should always have rain gear at the ready. Normally, I would have said that I was from here, too, but something in his eyes stopped me. I sensed he was going to say more, so I waited, and then he did.

"I was overseas for a while. I was in a lot of rain over there, and I told myself that if I ever made it out of there alive, I would never be out in the rain again unless I had to be."

I had the sense that this stranger was confiding in me, that he was telling me something important, but I struggled to figure out what that might be. Who would be out in the rain on purpose? And then I realized all kinds of people here were—hikers and mountain bikers, fishermen, kayakers, people who did not mind playing in the rain, who thought it was sort of fun, in a way, that it added to the sense of adventure. And so I said something about how crazy that was, about how no one in their right mind would be out in this on purpose, and then, by silent consensus, we headed out in the rain together—not running, just strolling.

My car was next to his, and we ambled along as if it were the sort of summer afternoon you dream of, like we were on a beach somewhere, and it was seventy-four degrees with a light wind, and later there would be cocktails and hors d'oeuvres and an impossibly beautiful sunset. And that's when it came to me—what he had been trying to say.

"Where were you overseas?" I asked, even though I knew the answer by then. I had intuited it, felt it in the thick air, pulled it out of the deep recesses of what I had read in books and seen in movies. He fixed his gaze on me, his eyes gray sheets of rain.

"Vietnam."

As we stood by our cars, I searched for something neutral to say, something that would acknowledge the hardness of it all without bringing it all back, though the rain had clearly done that already.

"I bet you've got stories," I finally said.

"Yeah. Yeah, I do," he said. And then he added, "But I don't tell them."

As soon as he said it, I realized how completely inane my response had been, as if he had been to a wild overseas party instead of a war.

"I'm sorry," I said, meaning both for my flippant comment and for the stories that kept him up at night. I saw that now—the dark circles under his eyes, the watchful way he waited before he spoke.

"Thank you," he said.

And that was it. We loaded our soaked groceries into our cars, then waved goodbye. By the time I got home, the rain had stopped, but it would be back, intruding on my summer, coming and going at will, testing my tolerance, my patience, my good-humoredness, my joy writing project, and while I waited out this rainiest of seasons, I thought of what it might have been like to be nineteen years old in Vietnam, all the horrible things you would see, just a kid, no hope of anything except one day getting out and going home so you could begin a lifetime of trying to forget it all.

Though I never caught the man's name, never asked for it, I have often thought of him since, about the story he trusted me with, the one he told without even telling it, about all of our stories, the ones we keep and the ones we share, about how our whole lives are simply stitched-together stories and how we are stitched together by stories too, you and I, and how all our stories are sacred, every single one—the easy ones, the complicated ones, the ones that haunt us and the ones that bring us joy.

I used to worry that writing in general (and memoir writing in particular) was a frivolous pursuit, all that turning inward, all that going back in time and trying to make sense of things, wondering how to make things right when you can never really go back, never really change what was. But now? Now I believe the wondering itself is a form of prayer and that listening to other people's stories, witnessing their pain and sorrow, is too. And so I hold these stories—mine and yours and his and ours—in my hands, turning them over and over again, listening for all the things we cannot yet say, all the things we may never be able to say, searching for the whispers between the words—the holy parts.

6

SPICE UP YOUR LIFE

A MONTH AFTER the Supreme Court overturned *Roe v. Wade*, after the collective sigh we uttered after Trump left office and COVID vaccines were plentiful and investigations into the attack on the Capitol began, my husband, three of our adult children, my mother, and I waited to hear Dvořák's *Symphony No. 8* on the music-center lawn. Six people. Five folding chairs. A picnic blanket. A collapsible table. Two coolers. Four bottles of wine—cabernet, pinot grigio, sparkling rosé, a red blend. A picnic backpack full of plastic wine glasses and cloth napkins and plates, a miniature cutting board, utensils, a wine opener.

The main feature, however, was a charcuterie board made by a woman who, according to one of my friends, once worked for Victoria Beckham. Who knows whether this was actually true? But my friend had sounded sure, so I repeated it to everyone in our party as if it *were* true, and soon I found myself thinking of this as a Spice Girls cheese board. Very nineties. Very posh. A Spice Up Your Life cheese board.

As we poured wine and took turns heaping cheese and crackers and fruit and nuts onto our plates, the open-air auditorium filled, the violinists began warming up, and the conductor came on stage. Dvořák's symphony would be the second half of the performance. The first half was a symphonic tutorial where we reviewed the various sections and how they contributed to the overall sound. Something about woodwinds. Something about percussion. I tried to follow along, but I was increasingly distracted by the family in front of us.

Four girls, ranging in age from maybe four or five to twelve or fourteen, one boy around eight or nine, and their mother all sat on towels spread out like blankets. The towel edges, perfectly aligned, touched but did not overlap. The father sat to the left of his family, not in a lawn chair but in one of those colorful plastic chairs you often find in preschool classrooms. The mother, maybe five or six months pregnant, had beautiful olive skin and strong cheekbones. She was petite and yoga-y. Perfect posture. Perfect composure. The taut muscles in her back rippled through her light cotton dress, and her girls all had similar poise and similarly styled and patterned dresses. The boy matched his father—blue pants, short-sleeve cotton dress shirt.

I was staring. I knew I was. It was a terrible habit. I did it in train stations and in airports, in line at the grocery store, across crowded restaurants. Still, I couldn't help myself. Blame the wine or the music or the suffocating summer heat, but the gorgeously calm mother, the eerily unmoving children, were an artful arrangement of dots on canvas, not a real family but an impression of a family—*A Sunday Afternoon on the Island of La Grande Jatte*. The illusion was so complete that when the youngest girl leaned against her mother and the mother's back muscles ever-so-slightly tensed, I gasped. The painting had shifted.

At intermission, no one in our party moved. We were in Van Gogh Alive, a multisensory exhibit with light and words and sound and scent. Above us, swallows dove, then rose once again into the trees. In the grass beside us, a standard poodle stalked a bunny. We poured more wine, passed around homemade cookies and pistachio toffee. The mother in front of us broke her pose long enough to hand snacks to her children: Ritz crackers, a bowl of Bear Naked granola, insulated water bottles. During all of this, the only time the father spoke was to lean forward and correct the boy who, after the first hour, went from sitting to lying on his towel. With a jerk of the father's head, the boy sprang upright again. As the symphony began, the sun dipped behind the mountains. Fireflies flickered through the field. The mother and children returned to stillness, but who is to say whether they were moved?

The whole country felt like it was divided that summer, frozen in place and time. We were sort of post-pandemic and sort of not, sort of post-Trump and sort of not. We were stuck in the in-between, and things could just as easily go one way as another. Perhaps this is the reason that for days afterward, I thought of those girls, their eerie silence, their father's icy calmness, and though I did not exactly believe in prayers, not in the way many people did, I sent out my own form of blessings to those children, deep, fulsome wishes to no one in particular and to the whole universe at once. *May the Lord bless and keep you. May his countenance shine upon you. May you grow into fullness and loud, boundless joy. May you someday be what you wannabe. In the name of Ginger and Sporty and Scary and Baby and Posh. Amen.*

7

THE BEAUTY OF THE *F* WORD

MY DAUGHTER WAS living in an eighth-floor apartment in New York when she adopted what the rescue organization claimed to be a house-broken adult dog—small enough to fit in a carrier on an airplane or on the subway but not so small that you might accidentally sit on her and squish her. Twenty-two pounds, white with black spots and a black patch on one eye, Aida was adorable and sweet and full of personality. She was perfect—well, *almost.*

As Aida grew . . . and grew . . . and grew, she chewed clothes, furniture, shoes—you name it. She still smelled like a puppy and breathed like a puppy. In the midst of a game of catch or tug-of-war, she would suddenly keel over and fall into a deep, dream-filled sleep as only puppies can do. The oddest thing, however, was that she insisted on peeing in the shower, a fact Alex discovered when, well, Aida jumped in the shower and peed. She did this again and again, even after they had walked for miles, even after she had been to doggy day care and the dog park, even after Alex stalked another peeing dog, then showed Aida an example pee: *Look. This is how it is done.* It was becoming clear that *housebroken* was a subjective term, as was *adult.*

However, eventually Alex concluded that Aida had been *trained* to pee in the shower, which, correct me if I'm wrong, might be a city thing, but what would I know? I have only raised country dogs, most recently hounds who admittedly have some flaws, but shower peeing isn't among them. Anyway, after weeks of trying to retrain Aida during a frigid New York winter, Alex began to reconsider her hardline policy against indoor urination. Standing on a busy New York City sidewalk and begging a dog to please, *please* pee was both discouraging and embarrassing. On the other hand, shower pee was easy to clean and did not require braving blizzard-like conditions or public humiliation. Finally, Alex came around to Aida's way of seeing things. No more carrying the dog down the elevator and pacing up and down the dark street in the middle of the night. No more frantic googling about how to get a dog to pee outside. No more planning the daily schedule around the remote possibility that the dog might decide to pee normally, by which I mean like every other dog on the planet.

"Oh, what the fuck," Alex finally said.

Not an admonition—not *What the fuck is she doing?*—but a surrender: Why the hell not? What harm was it really doing? They still walked for exercise, still went to the dog park for socialization, but shower peeing became not the *preferred* method but an *acceptable* method, a viable option. By early summer, because Aida was pushing thirty pounds, far beyond the airline's weight limit for carry-on dogs, Alex drove her from New York to our home in North Carolina. Within moments of her arrival, she promptly announced that the dog needed to use our shower.

"You've got to be kidding me," I said. "Is she still doing that?"

She was indeed, and though I at first balked at the idea of their bringing their zany city ways here to the woods, where there were so many options for outdoor peeing—a zillion trees or leaf piles or grassy areas or bushes or mossy outcroppings—within a couple of days, I, too, had recalibrated and readjusted my expectations. Even my husband, who, gesturing wildly to the fifty-three wooded acres surrounding our cabin, had at first vowed to train this dog to pee outside if it were the last thing he did, finally acquiesced. Before long, he, too, was pulling back the shower curtain and whipping out the bleach bottle while Aida crossed her little legs and nervous-danced on the bath mat.

"This is fucking ridiculous," he said when she jumped in and peed, then hopped out and waited for us to rinse the tub and wipe her paws.

"Give her a treat!" Alex called from the other room.

Pretty soon, we were relinquishing all the country hound-dog methodology that had served us well in training our own dogs. Instead, we were routinely allowing, maybe even sometimes *encouraging*, this aberrant behavior. *Fuck it*, we too now said, giving up and giving in, embracing what I now thought of as the Fuck-It School of Thought, which seemed beautiful and transcendent in a way, like the word *fuck* itself (which, incidentally or perhaps significantly, my grammar check keeps flagging as "offensive"). With its soft and gentle beginning, the guttural moan in the middle, the hard and certain finale, *fuck*, like a well-whipped cream, folds seamlessly into other phrases, expressions of delight or outrage or despair like, *That's so fucking awesome* and *fuck, no* and *fuck, yeah* and *fuck me* and *fuck that* and *fuck off* and *Are you fucking kidding me?*—bright bursts of celebration or passion or astonishment or reclamation, a way of calling attention to and calling forth, an almost spiritual revelation, not unlike the notion of letting go and letting God. This made me consider how if you release one way of looking at things, you might make room for another, the way good things might creep up on you like a black snake while you're dozing on a lawn chair in your yard.

You wake from a dead sleep, and—*Oh, fuck!*—there she is stretched in the grass at your feet, her sleek body a ripple of waves, her tongue flickering in the warm air. Her presence is unexpected, sure, maybe even shocking, but she is also radiant and lovely, and seeing her there makes you a little radiant and lovely too, a little more alive than you had felt just moments before, and perhaps then you say it again—*Oh, fuck*—only now the words are softer and gentler, like you.

At this moment in my life, the number of fucks I have to give is infinitely smaller than it was when I was younger, and the list of things I have given up caring about is extensive. For example—and I can't even believe I'm even writing this now—a number of years ago, I did a medically supervised weight-loss program, and based on the advice of my nutritionist, I actually *weighed the apples I ate* ("A typical apple is *not* four ounces," she had cautioned, circling "four-ounce apple" on the list of fruits I would be allowed). She also suggested I dilute my wine with—get this—sparkling water, which seemed almost sacrilegious. *Fuck that*, I thought then, and I think it even now.

But that's the thing: If you ever once start stopping giving a fuck, it becomes a slippery slope, a "one-way ticket," as my dad used to say when, as a teenager, I got caught sneaking out with my hard-partying boyfriend. I suppose my dad meant that if you go down certain roads, you are in for all sorts of trouble, and looking at that boy and me here, forty years later, I think perhaps my father was right. In any case, since turning fifty-five, I have disavowed all sorts of things—bleaching my hair, making polite conversation, counting my steps, giving my time to people I don't enjoy, low-carb diets, working for for-profit organizations for free, answering work emails on weekends. *Fuck all that*, I have said in one way or another. And as I have purged my life of the things that deplete my energy and zap my joy, all sorts of wondrous things have crept in—new friendships, new professional opportunities, new flavors of Ben and Jerry's, and on and on and on.

I recently read a CNN report on the benefits of swearing that cited a study that found a strong correlation between cursing and verbal intelligence—a positive correlation, that is. The article also claims that knowing when it's okay to swear and when it's not may also mean swearers in general have relatively high levels of social intelligence. Relative to what, you may ask? I do not know. But I think we should take good news when we can, so I'm taking it. The article also cites other studies suggesting that profanity may help with endurance training and pain tolerance, and—get this—may also be a sign of creativity. *Fuck, yeah.*

The same report references researcher Emma Byrne, who in her recent book, *Swearing Is Good for You: The Amazing Science of Bad Language*, says that cuss words lodge in the right side of our brains along with all our other creative impulses like our desire to do sip and paint or throw clay pots or make a batches of soap or cut our own bangs. Well, she doesn't say that *exactly*, but that's the gist of it. She also says cussing can help us *calm the fuck down* (again, I'm paraphrasing) and that, because it is often associated with strong emotions, profanity may also last in a person's memory long after other words have faded.

The idea that we remember longest what we have most loved, hated, feared, and desired seems like a no-brainer, and I am delighted to know that some of my most precious memories—of falling in love, of my babies being born, of biking and hiking and running, of boisterous family dinners and lazy beach trips with friends—are lodged there right among my *what the hells*, and *oh, shits*, and *for fuck's sakes*. It is enough to make you reevaluate what you consider divine, by which I mean delightful and true. (The word *divine* always conjures for me that sugary, glossy white candy I sometimes make at Christmas but only at Christmas and now I wonder why that is, why one never makes divinity in July, for example, which again is the slippery slope of reseeing. What if, for example, we served divinity each year on the Fourth of July right alongside hot dogs and potato salad and watermelon? What new things might we then imagine? Who might we then become?)

This is the power of the Fuck-It School of Thought, the way one thing becomes another when examined in a slightly different light, the way the many layers of being unfold right in front of you. Here is a case in point: When our kids were younger, my friend Lisa and I used to have a running joke in which we referred to Sunday morning sex as "going to church." I can't remember how this started, but we found it hilarious. One of us might say, "Sorry I didn't call you sooner. I was at church," and the other one would crack up and say, "Me too! I went to church this morning too!" There were all sorts of variations on the joke, additions and asides, such as, "Well, did you stay for Sunday school?" or "How was the sermon?" or "Did the choir sing?" so many, in fact, that I often lost track of what precisely we were referencing.

Still, every single time, we thought it was funny, and lately, I've begun to wonder whether this, too—lying in bed with your lover on a Sunday morning, yes, but also the act of sharing this delight with a friend, of saying, I see you there, working your job, raising those kids, six days a week running them to this activity and that one, cooking their meals and doing their laundry and supervising their homework and entertaining their friends and loving them and worrying over them, doing all you can to make their lives good, and I am happy you have one morning a week to linger in bed with your beloved, and even though you can still hear kids fighting, cartoons blaring, the dog chasing the cat up and down the stairs, there in the bedroom, the light streams through the window and warms the walls, the sheets, your hair, and in that moment, *holy fuck* (an interjection) might even rise to the occasion of *holy fuck* (an adverb and a verb), a consecrated and sanctified act.

In this way, then, *fuck* (the word, not the act, but maybe that too) becomes a punctuation mark, an almost reflexive conclusion, an exclamation mark, a rallying cry or even a mantra and not all that far from a prayer in my mind, a way of being in the world, not careless or detached but honoring what is good and releasing all the rest, like saying *God love him* or *bless your heart*, which, here in Appalachia, means we see your imperfections and raise you our own imperfections, our own flawed humanity, which is all to say that there are as many ways to offer gratitude for this life as there are souls in this world and beyond. So *fuck yeah* to there's still time and *fuck no* to wasting any of it and *don't fucking get in my way* while I'm out here killing it, better *fucking* late than never.

8

GIN AND BEAR IT

ONE SUMMER DAY after a year of post-pandemic teaching, Lisa and I met for early morning coffee and a walk around the lake by her house. And by coffee I mean gin. Chocolate orange gin liqueur from an Asheville distillery, to be exact. The first shot was *just to taste it.* The second was a *follow-up taste.* Followed by a couple of *actual shots.* We drank them in tiny red plastic cups, shot-sized Solo cups, and when we were finally ready to go on our walk, we each took a tiny cup with us. *For hydration.*

Lisa and I were both sixties-era babies, and by some odd coincidence, we both had the middle name Dawn, an upbeat, optimistic name. The dawning of a new age. The dawn of time. Darkest before the dawn. And so on. We had known each other for over twenty years, and the past year of teaching (elementary school for her, college for me) had been brutal. We were depleted and disillusioned, ready for career changes but too old and set in our lives to hope for any meaningful change. We had entered what we feared was the grin-and-bear-it stage, or perhaps more aptly, the gin-and-bear-it stage, which necessitated a bit of leeway in terms of when summer happy hour officially began.

It was late July, the air thick with bees and gnats and no-see-ums. A layer of pollen coated the lake, and the dank smell of fish mixed with the gin/orange/chocolate aroma. We hadn't seen each other since the previous summer when, in the midst of a thunderstorm, we had eaten pizza huddled under umbrellas in my driveway due to COVID. Now, strolling and sipping, we talked about everyone we knew who was leaving education, of all the reasons we might leave, of how we would leave if it weren't for retirement and health insurance and so on.

It had been such a rough year. All the administrative bullshit. All the masking and the monitoring of masking. All the instruction students had missed. All the socialization. All the going-to-school skills. All the additional duties and responsibilities teachers had assumed with no commensurate compensation. The hopelessness of it all. The energy-zapping, creativity-sucking, mind-numbing nature of it all. One day in the future, we might feel optimistic again. We might even feel joyful again. But that was not where we were in this moment. We offered one another no solutions, no words of encouragement even, only companionship, and after twenty years of friendship, the rhythm was familiar, the cadence of this side-by-side walking that good friends do. The listening. The space giving. The witnessing. Our walk a meditation, a communion, a thanksgiving.

Sip.
Walk.
Talk.
Talk.
Walk.
Sip.
Repeat.
Repeat.
Repeat.

9

THE CHAIR OF THE SIDEWALK DEPARTMENT

WHEN I ARRIVED at the DMV at 10:00 a.m., a group was already lined up on the sidewalk like they were camping out for concert tickets. One woman, approximately my age, sat in a lawn chair. As soon as I got out of my car, she called to me.

"Hey! Hey! Do you have an appointment?"

I couldn't tell what answer she wanted, so I hesitated before indicating that I did indeed.

"That's good," she said.

But her tone indicated it was anything but good. She had been here since 7:15 a.m. She was next in line. But if I had an appointment, that was another story. She would have to wait. It was the sort of pronouncement where the *fuck you* at the end was implied. *I will wait. Fuck you.* When I reached the office door, though, it was locked, the glass covered with signs indicating you were not to attempt to open it. You were to wait for your turn. The process was a holdover from height-of-the-pandemic protocol, and though most offices had by now moved back to business as usual, it was a bit surprising but not completely unfamiliar. As I stood outside the door, two more people (customers? Were we customers? Clients? Suppliants? Petitioners?) arrived.

"Do y'all have an appointment?" the lawn-chair woman asked each of them.

They each obligingly answered, as if this woman held some sort of power, as if in laying claim to that sidewalk square, she was now block captain or neighborhood watch chairwoman. The Chair of the Sidewalk Department. One of the customers, a man I guessed to be in his late eighties, said he just needed to return one piece of paperwork. Lawn-Chair Woman interrupted.

"I'm sorry, but you're not getting in front of me."

"We'll just see what the guy says."

The rest of the sidewalk waiters silently watched this play out, a mildly entertaining distraction, then returned to their snacks and activities. Coffee. Bagels. Games on their phones. One guy's phone rang with the "Wagon Wheel" ringtone, and everyone grew silent. I was trying to figure out whether it was the Old Crow version or the Darius Rucker version when Lawn-Chair Woman interjected her approval.

"That's a good song."

We all nodded at her proclamation and stood silently as the guy answered his phone. Something about proof of insurance. Something about a fax. Then one woman got up and rapped on the DMV office door. Finally, a man came to open it.

"Can I use the bathroom? I really need to use the bathroom."

When he let her in, we all gasped.

"I don't know why they don't hire more people," Lawn-Chair Woman said. "I would work here. All you have to do is sit on your butt and punch a bunch of keys."

She looked at me, but I felt awkwardly privileged with my appointment, so I stared silently at the door, willing it to open so I could escape the sidewalk scrutiny. Finally, the DMV official came back out with a clipboard. He was calling names. The names of people with appointments: the older man, the "Wagon Wheel" man, and, mercifully, me. The others watched as we strolled into the waiting room. When the door shut behind us, I was relieved.

Lawn-Chair Woman reminded me a bit too much of some of my high school classmates, the ones who had seemed rough around the edges, so to speak, who walked around with chips on their shoulders, always up for a confrontation, a showdown. What I am trying to say is that I was reminded of the kids who used to bully me in high school, though we didn't call it bullying then. We didn't call it anything because it was so commonplace, so expected in the community I grew up in, with its vast economic and cultural divides (even then). With no language to express or explore or understand what I was experiencing, I didn't think to wonder where those shoulder chips had come from. I simply felt the wrath of those I'll-beat-your-ass-you-stuck-up-bitch kids as I passed them on the breezeway.

Now, however, if I had to guess, I would have said the divide between them and me—a kid just one generation removed from the sort of lives many of them had, a kid whose father had fought his way out of poverty and had, on his own dime and by his own will, earned the master's degree that had gotten him a management job at the local film and paper plant and had in turn secured my future, ensured that I could go to college loan-free, debt-free—had something to do with education and opportunities, which is to say, it might have been reduced to or exemplified in who knew how to book online appointments and who had the foresight to keep a lawn chair in their car. Both of those now seemed like equally important life skills, only in this scenario, the former was a bit more helpful, and now I was old enough to feel some sense of . . . not shame, exactly, not embarrassment, exactly, but something approaching humility, an awareness of my privileged position, which in turn made me consider how hard it must have been to sit in a lawn chair and watch everyone else parade past you as if you were not there, as if you had not been there all along.

In the office, the three men and I sat in chairs spaced six feet apart, and I was so lost in my own thoughts that I almost did not hear the DMV officer call my name, but when he said it a second time, I leapt up. In the back room, I was photographed, my passport and driver's license examined, and then the examiner (who had said upon looking at my driver's license, "Oh, we were born the same year!" though he looked a decade younger than I did) wanted to know what hair color I wanted on my brand spanking new state ID that would allow me to fly on an airplane (or, according to the DMV website, visit a nuclear facility).

"I see you have some gray and some brown. Which one do you want me to put?"

I waffled.

"You choose. Either one."

Neither the gray nor the brown I currently had was actually my own. It was my hair stylist's best attempt at "smoky gray," a color I found on a L'Oréal color box and photographed to show him. As a young child, I had been blond. Then, as I got older, my hair had turned brown, and when I was still in my twenties, I started turning gray. Over the years, I had colored it many different shades, including brown, red, brownish red, reddish brown, purple, mauve, cool blonde, and so on. Once I had let a stylist dye a white streak down the side like a skunk. My coarse hair didn't hold any color for long, though, and within a couple of weeks after coloring, it reverted to its original state, its default color, as I had come to think of it: gray-gray.

Reality, in terms of my hair but in terms of other things, too, like who was a bully and who was not, like who had the upper hand and who did not, was constantly morphing and shifting. In this moment, though, I could determine for the record what was most real, what was most true. It was oddly unsettling. Heads, I was gray. Tails, I was cool blond. Whatever that was.

The examiner waited quietly.

"Gray," I said after what felt like a long pause.

"You're going with gray?"

His fingers were poised above the keyboard, like a fairy who could, with a few strikes of a wand, make me young again. It was tempting, to be sure, but being young is only fun if you do not know that you are young, and the very second you start trying to get back there, it's too late. You're already gone. If I could go back now, it would not be the same. *I* would not be the same.

"Yes," I said. "I'm sure."

He held my gaze for another second before returning to his tap-tap-tap-tapping. And just like that, we were done. He escorted me to the door, and upon exiting, I was back on the sidewalk, where no one had moved an inch. It felt wrong to walk past without comment, so I called to the group, perhaps a bit too cheerily, "Good luck, y'all!"

Lawn-Chair Woman thanked me, but not in a friendly way, more in a half-hearted, defeated kind of way, which I now could sort of see. Then, as I was almost to my car, I heard a woman sitting on the sidewalk telling the group around her that when she was fourteen years old, a group of Marines had come to their house and dragged her dad out of bed and into the backyard in the middle of the night. Suddenly, I wanted to stay, to sit in the warm sunshine and eat bagels and drink coffee with a woman who had such a story to tell, to spend time doing what I had never done when I was younger, a natural brunette who had no time for other people's stories, no interest in learning what made people who they were, but it seemed rude to linger, voyeuristic, even, so I waved to everyone, and everyone waved to me, and for all I know, they are all still sitting there today

waiting . . .

waiting . . .

waiting to be called.

10

MIXED MESSAGES

TRAIL RUNNING ONE steamy Sunday summer morning in DuPont Forest, I had just climbed the last big hill of my four-mile loop and was in the home stretch, the relatively easy half mile back to the parking lot. My headphones were cranked up, and I was in my zone, jamming out to Tyler Childers's "Way of the Triune God"—the hallelujah version—when I encountered two men walking just ahead of two women. As I ran past, one of the men called to me. I slowed and turned down my music.

"Why don't you just take your shirt off?" the man hollered.

Now, I realize that this sounds pretty offensive, pretty inappropriate, and it struck me that way too at first. *Fuck off*, I almost said. *Asshole.* The old me would certainly have said it, but the new me, the one who was intent on tracking down joy, the one who was working on being nicer in general and to tourists I met on the trail more specifically, hesitated. Then I considered continuing as if I hadn't heard him. But the man was maybe in his early seventies, and he had such a friendly smile, and his wife was right there behind him, smiling and waving too, so I paused for a second.

Through my headphones, I could still hear Tyler singing. My playlist lately had been a combination of eighties pop and rock, classic country, bluegrass and newgrass and Americana mixed with sixties protest music—AC/DC, ABBA, Queen, Janis Joplin, Nina Simone, Willie Nelson, Mavis Staples, Old Crow Medicine Show, the Steeldrivers, Arlo Guthrie, Bonnie Raitt, John Prine, Patti Smith, the Dead, The Band. It also included gospel music—old-time tunes, mainly, but also a few contemporary spirituals songs by preachers, ex-preachers, activists, stoners, cons and ex-cons, poets, misfits and do-gooders, so many different voices all searching for truth in one way or another just as I was on this trail on a Sunday morning, the woods my church, my refuge from the noise of the world.

Thirty-one years old, the son of a coal miner, Tyler Childers was raised in Kentucky. "The Way of the Triune God" is from his latest album, *Can I Take My Hounds to Heaven?* The album contains three different versions of eight songs, the hallelujah, the jubilee, and the joyful noise versions. This grouping of threes is perhaps a musical nod to the Holy Trinity, and "The Way of the Triune God" is a tribute to old-time religion, to a screaming-and-shouting type of religious fervor. In the song, the speaker is filled with a sense of purpose, and the result is a jubilant song, a celebration of life and faith and the promise of a hereafter. I was not conventionally religious, but that in no way interfered with my love for his music or for gospel music in general.

Tyler's music offered a powerful antidote to my angst, my anxiety, my annoyance, so when the stranger on the trail called to me, I suppose Tyler was working his usual magic, mellowing me out, filling me with the Holy Spirit as only he could do because watching the man's face, all flushed and good-natured, it occurred to me that perhaps he had meant the comment nicely, in a *noncreepy* way, maybe even sympathetically, with genuine concern, like, you look really hot, not *sexy hot*, mind you, more like you're about to have a stroke, and maybe you would feel better if you threw off that T-shirt that is obviously weighing you down, a sentiment I bet even Tyler might have embraced—not the throwing-off-the-shirt part but the getting-rid-of-dead-weight part.

So there I was, filled with the Holy Spirit or at least Tyler's spirit, but also exhausted, ready to be finished with my run and not in the mood to chat with anyone, friendly or otherwise, because I came to the woods to be alone, to think my own thoughts, but here I was. Here we both were. The man was waiting for me to respond, and finally I decided on something neutral:

"It sure is hot today."

"Yeah, yeah, it is," he said, as if nothing at all awkward had just transpired.

The other man and the women nodded in agreement, and there we all were, commiserating and wishing one another well:

> *It's a scorcher!*
> *Be careful!*
> *Have a good one!*

No one was more astounded than I at this unlikely turn of events. As sweat poured down my cheeks, purifying me, sanctifying me, stinging my eyes, soaking my neck and my sports bra, my shirt so drenched I would wring it out when I got home, I pressed rewind on my Apple Watch, and Tyler began again, as we all so often do, as I was doing even now, and in my own way, I sang along: May I be of use. May my body be of service. May my joyfulness take your kindness and raise you one. Way up here on the mountain, where all such things are possible.

11

FOLLY

DURING A TRIP with two high school friends to Folly Beach in South Carolina, I was heading out for a run one afternoon when one of the girl-women—we were all girl-women that weekend—complimented my calves.

"You certainly win in that category," Helen said.

I had always been self-conscious about my bulky calves. I was constantly bunching them up and stuffing them into knee-high boots and slim-fitting jeans, like sausages in leather casings, so when Helen of the perfectly proportioned calves and the perfectly flat stomach (*still*—at our age) complimented them, I was flattered. Helen never exercised and was at that moment kicked back in a lounge chair, a vodka tonic balanced on one thigh. She wore several David Yurman necklaces tastefully layered and a white string bikini.

I understood, of course, that Helen meant she considered my legs to be fine *for a woman my age*, an important caveat. She meant it generously, though, and this compliment coming from Helen, who, of the three of us, was most attuned to such matters, was high praise indeed, so I thanked her and felt awesome for approximately three minutes, until I began to more closely analyze the tone in which her proclamation had been delivered: you certainly won in *that* category. *That* category, presumably, being the leg category or maybe just the calf category, but in any case, the phrasing brought to mind the question of what the other categories were and in which ones I had not come out on top.

"I had a facelift, so I don't have all that," Helen had said the day before as she leaned in to inspect the loose skin on my neck.

Though I looked like the late-middle-aged woman I was, the mother of three grown children, Helen looked much like she had back in high school—thin, long blond hair, suntanned. She meant to be helpful, like, *Hey, not to worry. That's totally fixable. Let me hook you up with my plastic surgeon.* On one hand, this advice left me worried I was falling apart. Considered another way, however, it meant I had potential, that the illusion of time standing still was still possible, that if I could just come up with a spare ten grand, I would be all set, *good to go.*

The very fact that I did not even consider asking for the surgeon's number or trying to figure out how I might come up with that kind of money, that instead I laughed when she said it, that we all laughed about how weird this all was, how hard it was to be both sixteen and fifty-five at the same time, for it to be both 1984 and 2022, was a sign of maturity. But here we were, once again day-drinking, living on takeout pizza, riding our bikes into town a bit too unsteadily, leaning a bit too hard into our eighties retrospective.

Our companion into this foray into the past was a foster dog, an elderly, terminally ill poodle Helen had rescued a couple of weeks before. The dog had seizures every couple of hours and had to be revived with honey, so each afternoon after Buddy and Helen woke up, the three of us carted the dog down to the beach, and whenever he flopped over on the sand, temporarily paralyzed from the neck down, we revived him with spoonfuls of honey. *It's okay, Buddy*, we said. *We've got you, Buddy*—the name itself an endearment. Eventually, he came around, stood, then wandered around sniffing the air and digging in the sand while Angela and I sipped beer and Helen sipped vodka with a splash of water or not, just like the good ol' days, before we all three went our separate ways, more or less.

Anyway, all that winning, all the going back in time, all that trying to catch up on the last twenty-five years, the talk of what had happened to such-and-such and so-and-so, one too many of us gone or almost-gone or might-as-well-be-gone, was dizzying, and while Angela and Helen talked, I tilted my head back, dug my toes into the cool sand, listened to their voices blending with the surf. Winning in one category, I understood, meant losing in another.

Buddy, for example, was a winner in that he had been adopted, that he had gained a few good months before Helen flew off to an extended vacation on the Amalfi Coast. Then, I suppose, he would be losing again. There you go. Winning and losing, losing and winning, all intertwined, just like the way Helen and Angela and I had all survived the eighties—eyelash curlers, French jeans, Quiet Riot and AC/DC and Bon Jovi, wild boys and bathtubs of Purple Jesus—just to arrive here with our body parts still intact or tacked back on or plumped up or smoothed out, the waning afternoon sun and this time together a spoonful of honey, resurrecting the memory of the us we used to be.

12

EIGHTIES EXPERTISE

IN THE TRADER Joe's checkout line, the cashier and bagger, two twenty-something guys I knew in that way you know the people you routinely see in your day-to-day life, debated the virtues or lack thereof of the B-52's song "Love Shack."

"So what's the worst song from the eighties?" one of them asked me.

As he glanced meaningfully, expectantly at the other guy, it was clear that one of them thought "Love Shack" was the worst. The other one, however, thought it was amazing and had even perhaps been singing it right before I arrived on the scene. I'm pretty sure that the Trader Joe's cashiers are told, at least at the Asheville location, to make casual conversation with customers as they check out, so what seemed spontaneous may in fact have been the conversation starter of the day, but that did not make the question any less valid. Here was an opportunity: I could send "Love Shack" some love or declare it, with the authority invested in me by having been the only one of the three of us physically present in the eighties, the worst song of the decade.

However, I didn't want to take sides. These were the same guys who had given me free samples of iced peppermint lattes a few weeks before, the same ones who had recently helped me score the last bag of salsa verde chips. I didn't want to risk ruining our perfectly amiable relationship.

"That's hard," I said, nodding as emphatically and impartially as possible.

They scanned and nodded, shook out bags and filled them, talking and moving in equal time, a blur of twenty-something guy energy. The truth was, I hadn't given "Love Shack" much thought one way or the other. I mean, it had a catchy tune, but I didn't really get the lyrics, particularly that odd, out-of-nowhere line "Tin roof/rusted!" Originally, I had taken it as a code for *busted*, meaning the cops were on the scene, but I have since read that some people interpret it to mean that the woman in the romantic encounter is pregnant. Others, however, say that when Cindy Wilson delivered that line, she was just jamming along and ad-libbing, creatively playing, if you will. Seeing as how I love a good, upbeat tune, I thought "Love Shack" was, honestly, a perfectly fine song, but I kept my opinions to myself. One of the guys found my response unsatisfactory, however, and—I'm trying not to use the word *goaded* here—*pressed* me.

"I mean, there are so many bad eighties songs," one of them said.

Suddenly I was defensive about my generation's music. Sure, I constantly struggled to find a decent eighties playlist on Spotify, and even back in the eighties, I mainly listened to sixties music—the Stones, Zeppelin, The Who. Still, not *all* eighties music was bad. I mean, the eighties had given us Van Halen and Queen and Bon Jovi, Madonna and Cyndi Lauper and, hell, *Whitney Houston*. As I considered it, though, it came to me that I *did* have a particular disdain for Toto's "Africa," a tune writer Steve Almond has hilariously roasted for its obliviousness, its reductiveness and utter nonsense. (See *Tin House Magazine*'s tenth anniversary celebration in 2009 and Steve's 2010 book *Rock and Roll Will Save Your Life*.)

Recently, while strolling along a cliff in Dingle, Ireland, my daughter and I heard faint strains of music. The wind was strong, driving spitting rain sideways through the air. We were the only people in sight. We cocked our heads, listened harder, and finally followed the music to the edge of the rocky cliff. On a sandy outcropping below, a group of bathing-suit-clad teenagers lounged on towels. Next to them was a cooler and a set of portable speakers through which, you guessed it, "Africa" blared. No one seemed to care that the lyrics made no sense, that the song was essentially the word "Africa" with some drumbeats thrown in, not even here in Ireland, where you couldn't throw a rock without hitting someone playing a solid fiddle tune. The love that song had received over the years was, in my view, inexplicable.

"'Africa' was pretty bad," I said to the checkout guys.

One of the guys remembered how it went, but the other one didn't, so . . . what the hell? I sang a few lines, and they paused their frenetic bagging to listen, then nodded appreciatively before tossing my receipt in a bag and loading the bags into a cart. I thanked them and turned to leave, but as I was almost to the door, one of them called to me.

"What do you think of 'Purple Rain'?"

It was almost an afterthought. But the subject of the Artist Formerly Known as Prince was not one to take lightly. In my mind, Prince, seductive and subversive but also playful and prolific, embodied the best of the eighties. In fact, I had recently purchased a purple velvet jacket I liked to think of as my own personal fashion nod to Prince. "I'm channeling Prince," I said whenever I wore it. And I felt it, too, that intoxicating, colorful synergy too grand, too expansive to be contained in one human body, in one place and time.

"Prince was perfect!" I called back to the checkout guys as I strolled dramatically, confidently out the door.

The truth was, though, that with this dive into eighties music, these Gen Z checkout guys had sent me spiraling, as I was apt to do. I could go years without once thinking of one thing that happened between 1980 and the year my daughter was born, 1988. But then there I was, back in college, living in an apartment building not a half mile from this store, my roommate a girl raised on a Christmas tree farm way up in the North Carolina high country who said things like, "Yeehaw, we's wilder 'n a box of squirrels!" and "I'm stuffed as a tick!" My people were country but never *that* country, never that colorful. Missy and I used to sit on our cracked front stoop and drink straight Jack Daniel's and pass fat joints back and forth with the guy next door who had been critically injured in a car collision with a firetruck and whose brain was still recovering, still struggling to catch words and phrases and people from his past. We stayed there for hours, until the neighbor's psychotic cocker spaniel ran snarling and snapping at us, chasing us back inside. I failed every class I took that year except one— sociology—and some days I wondered what my life might be like now if I had not been so resigned to failure then, if I had looked ahead and seized all the possibilities before me instead of just sitting back and waiting for my life to begin.

The eighties had been a mixed bag for me, full of angst and uncertainty, but there had also been some sweet spots, some "tin roof/rusted" moments that may have been about getting laid or may have been about getting busted or may just have been me ad-libbing, digging, if you will, the moment. And as I further considered my exchange with the baggers, I realized it had been not so much a test as a celebration of their own eighties knowledge, a sort of checkout musical *Jeopardy!* where the only wrong answers were the ones you didn't give, the shots you didn't take, which seemed a lot like life itself. Right then and there, I made a promise to myself. In all future exchanges regarding eighties pop-music trivia, I would be undeterred and undaunted, unflinching and unafraid. I would not be usurped or undone or outwitted by two eighties pop-culture novices. No, sirs. Not me. I would be back next week for a Danish Kringle and a bag of ramen noodles, and I would be ready to impart some eighties musical wisdom.

Hit me with your best shot. *Fire away.*

13

HOT STUFF

ONE STEAMY AUGUST afternoon after a trail run, I stopped at a road-side produce stand near DuPont State Forest to buy tomatoes for the Bloody Mary salad I planned to make for dinner. As I squeezed one tomato after another to check for ripeness, I noticed an older man, maybe in his mid- or late seventies, sorting through the peppers. He wore a navy polo and khakis as if he had been golfing or might soon be golfing, which wasn't a wild guess since the store was across from a golf course. A few times I felt him watching me as if he had a question, but my dog was waiting in the car, so I chose the tomatoes I wanted and headed to the checkout line. Behind me, the man spoke. When I turned, he was waving a poblano pepper in the air.

"Hey," he said. "Does anyone know what this is?"

The question could have been for any of us—the cashier, the guy in line behind me, another woman sorting through potatoes. But he was looking at me.

"It's a poblano," I said.

The guy behind me, his arms full of corn—cradling the corn in the crooks of his arms, I mean—nodded.

"Oh," the man said. The pepper still dangled from his fingers. "What does it taste like? I mean, does it taste better than a bell pepper? Because those sort of taste like nothing."

I considered this for a moment. Did a bell pepper taste like nothing? I didn't think so, but then again I was no pepper expert.

"It has more of a bite than a bell pepper," I said, which we all considered for a few minutes.

Later, I realized *smoky* would have been the most apt descriptor, but, in fairness to me, I really didn't have adequate time to consider the question. The cashier and the guy behind me nodded in agreement, which the poblano man took to be a sign that we were on the right path.

"So what do you *do* with it?"

"It's good in Mexican food," I offered. "Or you could grill it. Or roast it in the oven."

"Huh," the man said, still not moving, not dropping the pepper.

He seemed to want us to elaborate, to offer something more along the lines of, *First, thoroughly wash the pepper, then slice it in half longways, leaving the stem and seeds. Then brush it with a tablespoon of olive oil, place on a baking sheet lined with aluminum foil, and broil until the surface is blistered. Then place it in a paper bag. When it is cool, peel off the charred surface. Then add to your favorite dish.*

At the time, I did not think to say this, but the person behind me said something—I could not hear the specifics—that tipped the scales in the poblano's favor because, finally, the man placed the pepper in his basket.

"Okay, okay," he said. "I'm going to try it."

"Great!" we all said. "Good idea!"

Later, at home, I told my daughter this story.

"Can you even believe that," I said in a way that wasn't a question. "What sort of man reaches that age without knowing what to do with a pepper?"

That second part actually *was* a question, and we debated the possibilities. A man whose wife always cooks dinner? But where was his wife? Was she dead? Had she left him? Had he left her, and his new, younger love interest didn't know how to cook? Or maybe he had a professional chef at home but was here on vacation. Or maybe he had dementia and had forgotten how to cook, had forgotten, even, the word *poblano*.

We went on and on trying to come up with a possible explanation, and every time we posited another possibility, a new version of this man emerged before me. He had the air of someone who had been in charge of things at one time. Maybe he had been in finance.

Maybe banking. Or stocks. Or perhaps he had been an engineer. Or a CEO of something. Or an administrator. Everything seemed possible. He was a CEO who had dementia and whose wife had just died. They got married as soon as they graduated from college, and she had stayed home to raise their three boys. That's why he didn't know how to cook peppers. And then, after the kids were grown, well, they were stuck in their roles. Day in and day out, he put on his suit and tie and went to the office, and she stayed home and . . . cooked peppers? Surely that wasn't all. Maybe she played tennis or canasta. Maybe she was a Master Gardener, or she volunteered for the local schools, or she was on the board of this or that. In the evenings, they sipped mint juleps or what-have-you in the garden next to the gardenia planter and talked about their days. Later, they ate grilled chicken and a salad with tomatoes and red onion and bell peppers. And then?

Admittedly, the picture was incomplete, but the point was, there was no more wife, no more gardenias. He was alone now, asking random strangers how to prepare basic produce, and though for a smoky-hot second I was completely annoyed with what seemed like gender stereotyping and all, the next moment I was simply grateful I had wandered in there, for all the possibilities he had conjured in me, for all the wonder his questions had raised in me, for all the wonders I had known and all that might still be.

14

DEER ROMANCE

ALONG A GRAVEL road in the Pisgah National Forest, an area my daughter and I have dubbed Coyote Pass (due to, well, the coyotes we've seen here), herds of deer spring from the thick brush on one side of the road, then disappear on the other side. Shadows, flickers, the suggestion of deer. I saw them often during the pandemic when the road was desolate. Then, as more and more people returned to the forest, I saw them less frequently and assumed the deer had headed farther back into the forest to escape the onslaught of humans. One day, though, in a spot where the trees gave way to sunlight, where animal tracks covered the soft ground, one solitary young deer sat in a thicket of vines and brush, his eyes the color of river mud. When he saw me, he calmly stood and sauntered away.

I didn't expect to see him again, but the next day, there he was, in the same place with the same unperturbed demeanor. This time, he looked at me longer, rose even more slowly, before disappearing into the forest behind him. Day after day, this continued, and each time we watched each other a little longer. Soon, I swore to anyone who would listen that this deer remembered me. The more I passed through, picking blackberries that sagged from the vines along the path, walking and running my dogs, the less skittish he became. He ran off the path, then paused a few feet away, legs quivering, his lovely brown eyes meeting mine. After a time, he stopped running from me altogether. He waited until I was within a couple of feet, then ambled off nibbling grass and weeds. *My deer*, I came to call him. "I saw my deer today," I would say. "I think my deer knows me now." Was he supposed to be on his own so young, or had something happened to his family? I had no idea.

Then, one day in mid-August 2021, the remnants of Tropical Storm Fred sent the Davidson River hurling from its banks. For days afterward, the forest was closed to nonessential workers, but on the news I watched videos of the destruction. In total, Fred dumped seventeen inches of rain on the region and caused more than eleven million dollars in damage. Some of the worst destruction was in nearby Cruso, just over the Haywood County line, where entire homes were washed down the Pigeon River. Six people died there. Dozens lost their homes and businesses. Closer to home, near the trail where I ran most days, where my deer lived, the Davidson River crested at fourteen feet. Surging from its banks, the water uprooted berry bushes, dragged sand and rocks and whole trees through the underbrush before spilling into the Job Corps parking lot on the other side of the woods. When I saw that image on the news, all the vehicles underwater, it was too much to take in, too much loss and destruction to process in the moment. And so I focused on my deer. He was so young, so alone. Would he have known to go to higher ground?

Trees had crashed into all three bridges leading to the nearby campground and hiking trails, so when the forest finally reopened, I ran along the main, paved road until a repair crew working on a bridge allowed me to cross onto the trail leading to Coyote Pass. There, the river had taken out whole banks and dozens of trees, and the earth had warped and buckled, as if an earthquake had hit. Part of the walking trail had collapsed into the river. A wooden footbridge had been catapulted down the trail, where it lodged against a rock. A logjam had blocked the river upstream a few miles, and the river was now shockingly low, the gutted riverbank exposed. The word *devastation* came to mind. The phrase *like a bomb went off*.

In light of this, the status of one deer did not seem of utmost importance, yet I was oddly obsessed with finding him. When I got to the clearing where I usually saw him, I stopped and considered what to do next. Should I call for him? That seemed absurd. But where might he have gone? I scanned the woods. Nothing. Not even the faintest rustling of leaves. But then, just when I was about to give up, off to my right, in the debris of blackberry bushes, something moved. I waited. Again, the slightest shifting of light and shadow. And then, finally, I could make out his outline. His soft, warm body made a deep impression in the vines, and as I got closer, his eyes met mine.

"Hello," I said. Ridiculously. "I'm so glad you're okay."

As he raised his head (a response?), I caught sight of something between his ears . . . a stick? A wound? And then he turned *just so,* and I realized he had the beginning of an antler. I had so many questions about where he had been, how he had been, but, of course, that was both the beauty and the difficulty of having a deer for a friend. It left a lot of room for speculation.

Six weeks later, I was walking one evening at dusk, and he once again strolled across my path, only this time he had not one but *two* distinct antlers, and he had something even better. In the bushes just beyond him, there was a rustling, and another deer appeared—a graceful beauty a shade darker, like the center of a buckeye—and I was filled with awe, yes, but also a joy that surprised me in its forcefulness. And because at this point in our relationship, I now regularly talked aloud to him, I said, "You have a girlfriend! How wonderful!"

Not only had my deer survived, but he had fallen in deer love, which I would like to believe is not all that different from human love, and the joy of seeing those two slip away into the woods together, a dip of his head in my direction that may have been real or may have simply been what I wanted to see, was pure magic, and the thrill of finding these two lovers, two survivors in the midst of so much devastation, was like nothing I had felt in a long, long time, maybe not ever.

15

WILLIES

ON A TOW path by a canal in Wales, I encountered a man who could best be described as dapper, which is not a word I throw around, but he was certainly that—gentlemanly in his tweed coat and hat—walking a small, chihuahua-*ish* dog. I was standing by the path watching the rest of my party complete a task that had, on day four or five of our narrowboating tour, become commonplace. We were moored by a filling station to top off our water tank so as to (1) maintain the supply to our boat and (2) keep the boat weighed down so it didn't scrape against the low-lying canal bridges.

The man was from a nearby village, which he named and which I promptly forgot as I was distracted by how adorably dignified the dog was, which is a bad habit of mine, the way people fade into the background whenever I see a cute dog. The dog's name was Louie (Louey? I didn't ask for the proper spelling, which I later regretted), and, though Louie/Louey acted very puppy-like, it turned out he was actually on the oldish side, which made me feel somewhat better about what happened next. In any case, Louie/Louey was very playful. I knelt down while he licked my face, and I rubbed his ears and his belly and told him how amazing he was, and after we chatted a few minutes, the man told the dog it was time to go. He tugged gently on the leash. However, Louie/Louey, leaning to one side, his, um, *private parts* engorged and spread out in the open for God and everyone to see, refused to move.

"Oh, no!" the man said. "His willie has come out!"

At this, he whipped from his pack a sling, like the ones used to swaddle infants.

"He does this sometimes," he said, now looking at us . . . apologetically? Expectantly? "Once his willie is out, he's done walking for the day, and I have to carry him."

Indeed, upon examination, I could see that, in relation to the size of the dog, the willie (if you will and if we must) *was* rather large—enough so as to inhibit walking, I would imagine, though I didn't have much experience in this area, so I couldn't say for sure. In any case, I didn't know whether to apologize for getting the dog overly excited or to reassure the man that this sort of thing happens, that it was perfectly okay and natural and nothing to be ashamed of, but neither he nor the dog seemed ashamed—more chagrined than embarrassed, I would say. Though it was somewhat awkward, I didn't want to come across as too uptight, too repressed, too *American*, so I chuckled, and the rest of my party—watching and listening more intently by the minute but also trying to act like they weren't because they, too, found it all ever-so-slightly awkward—chuckled, and when the man tucked the dog and his willie into his sling, he did it proudly, elegantly. I wished him a good day, and he tipped his cap and headed down the path, and we all stopped and watched the two of them stroll confidently, unabashedly away. Godspeed.

16

SUBJUNCTIVE MOOD

ON A LAZY, last-gasp-of-summer sort of day, I lingered on the patio of a south Asheville bakery. Leaning back in my chair, I marveled at the warmth, at the music drifting over from a nearby brewery, at my good fortune at having arrived here on what would have been, COVID notwithstanding, a perfectly normal Friday. Four days earlier, classes had begun at the university where I teach. Above their masks, my students were a cluster of startled eyes. In the long months we had been apart, we had forgotten one another, and the language with which I had learned to teach and they had learned to *student* no longer served us. An attendance policy? A late paper penalty? Ludicrous. COVID had shaped and shifted our narrative in ways we were just beginning to understand.

"Let's crack the windows," I had said. "So COVID can fly out the window."

Of course, this was not how COVID worked, but this was creative writing, not biology. Still, even with our fondness for words, we had no adequate way to articulate our sorrows, not the collective horrors or the smaller, everyday disappointments. Certainly, we couldn't refer to them in the simple past tense. Nothing was simply over. Past perfect tense was not helpful either: *Before the pandemic, we had . . .* What good did it do to remember what we did before? The future tense, too, was problematic: *This spring I will . . .* Who knew what would happen in the coming months? We could only speak definitively in the present tense, and first-person plural pronouns seemed most fitting: *we are unsure how to proceed.* And so we talked about our writing processes, about our fears and doubts and the struggle to begin.

"I'm afraid that what I write won't be good enough," one student said.

In the old days, I might have offered reassurances, but as it were (subjunctive!), I offered only validation.

"Oh, it won't," I said. "It absolutely won't."

What sort of teacher was I to discourage a blossoming young writer? What sort of person? Still, there it was, an inescapable truth: our words will never be enough. On one hand, it was liberating. If we accepted the inevitability of failure, we were free to flounder around on the page, finding beauty where we could. On the other hand, beauty was so fleeting. Nonetheless, we tried to capture snippets where we could. We were reading Ross Gay's *The Book of Delights*, and at the beginning of each class, we went around the room naming our delight for the day: A phone call from an old friend. A premium parking spot. A perfect cup of coffee. And now, for me, a new delight: Swedish crème.

"It's like cheesecake," the man at the counter had told me when I ordered. But the delicacy the server placed in front of me was as much like cheesecake as rain was like snow, as a flute was like a drum, which is to say that they vibrated differently in the body. Topped with strawberry puree, the thick custard I slurped from a spoon was creamy, yes, smooth, yes, comforting and familiar and exotic all at once—a moment unto itself. The crème glided down my throat, a heron landing on water, a sensation, a mood, and it was no longer late August, the leaves already beginning to turn, the air already crisp in the mornings, dusk coming earlier and earlier each day, but a random, uneventful spring day when nothing in particular was happening but everything was *about* to happen, daffodils dotting the hillsides, the morning air settling in your hips, midday sun humming with the promise of leisurely strolls and lakeside lounging, of outdoor concerts and sparkling rosé and charcuterie boards balanced on wobbly makeshift tables.

Each year, I mourned the passing of summer, that broad expanse of lazy days sandwiched between two demanding academic school years. Yet now I felt something else too, something akin to hopefulness for what was next, an eagerness to see what we might yet and even still and even though become. It was not the end of summer, the end of anything. The season of breathtaking, of basking, of rolling over on your back and exposing your pale, naked belly to the sun, had nearly arrived, the anticipation of which, in the way of things, was almost always sweeter than the thing itself, sweeter, even, than the memory of it all, which already surpassed my wildest expectations. I was not a reliable witness to anything, save the impotent beauty of words.

17

WILD THINGS

AS I WAS leaving my house to meet a friend for lunch, a mother possum carrying four babies on her back stopped in the middle of the gravel driveway. I did not immediately recognize her as a possum. In that moment, she could have been anything—a small deer, a big squirrel, or a turkey. I inched forward so as not to frighten her. As I did so, she also inched forward, or more like waddled or maybe even staggered under the weight of all those not-so-tiny babies, more like toddlers than infants, and as she made her way to the edge of the driveway, one head popped up. Two curious eyes. One pink nose. Four sets of paws and claws. And then another head. And another. And another. And another. Four heads. Eight eyes. Four noses. Sixteen hand/paws gripping or clutching or hanging or clinging or balancing . . . perfect technique and form, a gaggle of preschoolers holding onto a rope so no one gets lost.

I put the car in park and, grabbing my cell phone, slowly opened the door. The mother stumbled down the bank a few feet and waited, eyeing her offspring while the babies eyed me. With their beady/glassy gazes, they managed to look both menacing and adorable, stuffed animals with glued-on eyes. Of course, I had seen other possums. In fact, we routinely set up humane traps near our barn whenever it became apparent that uninvited guests had been visiting our henhouse. I was often the one who found the trapped animals—their wide, anxious eyes glimmering through the early morning fog. "We got one," I would text my husband, who would later put it in his truck, drive it to the gated development up the road, and release it. My father, who on occasion has been known to relocate a squirrel or two from his bird feeders to the national forest, found this ridiculous.

"You're not taking them far enough," he said. "They'll just come right back."

Which seemed impossible also. How big is a possum's territory? How long do the young stay with the mother? What does she teach them while they're there? How much does a baby possum weigh? These answers, too, were all knowable, of course, Google-able. Yet I preferred not to know, to revel in what seemed a great mystery.

Watching for snakes and turtles and newts and poison oak and whatever else might be in the woods, I crept down the bank, closer but not close enough to send the possum scurrying away. I took a dozen photos of essentially the same pose, the exhausted (annoyed?) mother (but perhaps I was projecting from my days of mothering three young children), the babies frantically clutching her back.

"You're safe here," I said when she curled into a *c* and fixed her gaze on me. "You're safe."

And then for a long time, we simply watched each other, human and marsupial, and if you have ever been lucky enough to be that close to a wild creature, you will know what I mean when I say that that there was something sacred and intimate and wild between this mama and her babies, and witnessing it felt like the most precious kind of gift, the kind you never see coming because who would ever have thought that baby possums riding on their mother's back—which, of course, all baby possums do—would seem so magical, so extraordinary? Who would ever have thought to wish to witness such a thing? No one. No one who was any good at wishing.

And yet.

And yet.

And yet.

18

WISHING

At a fountain on the Biltmore Estate, a young girl, maybe five or six with fiery red hair and a delphinium-blue dress, closed her eyes and tossed a coin into the basin. Her brother, a few years older and with equally blazing hair, observed from a few feet away. Wisteria blooms sagged from the trellis above. Behind them George Vanderbilt's 250-room French Renaissance château towered magnificently. The children were fairy-tale children, enchanting and enchanted, but as the girl prepared to toss in a second coin, the boy walked over and poked her shoulder.

"Don't bother making a wish," he said. "It won't come true."

Stop being such an asshole, I wanted to say. *Stop squashing her hope. Stop squishing her spirit.* Instead, I watched while the mother, standing nearby, rushed to intervene.

"Leave her alone," she told the boy.

The boy backed away. As I strolled past, the girl, unfazed, unperturbed, unconcerned, shrugged, tossed her last coin into the fountain, then skipped away with all her good, hopeful vibes, and I believed then what she must have believed—that, sure, whatever. The boy could be right. Wishes didn't always come true. They didn't even *usually* come true. But what if he were wrong, even once? What if she hoped for something big, and it came true—a cure for cancer, affordable housing for everyone, a resolution to the climate crisis, compassionate treatment for all those suffering from drug addiction, peace for families trapped in conflict zones around the world, true equality here at home? What if she believed those things were possible? What if we all did?

What if?

19

REVISION

THOUGH I WOULDN'T choose banana pudding out of a dessert lineup, so to speak, I have always liked the basic recipe printed on the box of Nabisco Nilla Wafers. (The cookies used to be called simply vanilla wafers, but Nabisco shortened the name back in 1967, the year I was born, which is beautiful symmetry, maybe even a sign, if you believe in such things.) In my book, as desserts go, banana pudding is not a ten but not a zero either, maybe a six. Though I rarely make it myself, when someone else does I enjoy it until the meringue gets soggy or the bananas turn brown or the whole thing takes on a strong alcohol taste, a big bowl of banana alcohol, at which point I feed it to my dogs or chickens because, although banana liqueur is perfectly good, no one wants Nilla Wafers in their booze.

My ambivalence toward banana pudding changed when, on a trip to New York, I visited Magnolia Bakery. The bakery makes other puddings—apple pie, red velvet, cold brew banana, and so on—but their banana version evokes for me southern potlucks and church suppers, only better, a new and improved version of the old staple. Not layered but stirred and served in a cup, more custard than pudding (though I'm not sure I know the difference), the dessert is rich and comforting and, most importantly, decidedly unsoggy. (I suspect this has something to do with the three cups of whipping cream and can of sweetened condensed milk that replace the milk in the original recipe, but I could be wrong.)

After I tried it, I told anyone who had ever served me anything with bananas or anyone I had ever witnessed eating a banana how good it was until finally my friend O. J. found the recipe online and sent it to me. It wasn't complicated, and it tasted pretty much like what I had eaten in New York, which is to say, amazing. My confidence in my dessert-making ability soared. Then, in a strange banana-related coincidence (among, believe it or not, a string of banana-related coincidences, as one of my students had just completed delivering a multimodal presentation on banana farming all while dressed in a banana costume), a colleague happened to mention in passing that he had discovered the best-ever recipe for banana pudding.

Still on a culinary high from my Magnolia pudding success, I scoffed and guffawed, but he was insistent, and, to be fair, he had in the past worked at a cheesecake factory (as in, a production facility, not the restaurant). Once he had even brought me proof of his culinary prowess: an incredibly creamy slice of his homemade cheesecake. What I'm saying is, he had a good baking track record, so I was inclined to take him and his banana pudding seriously. When he later sent me his recipe, therefore, in return, I sent him my recipe—the Magnolia recipe, that is. *Game on.*

His recipe, it turned out, was from Paula Deen, which was, of course, problematic. Or, rather, I found Deen herself to be problematic. I was still undecided on her pudding. Though I had occasionally used her recipes in the past, after the 2013 scandal during which she had admitted to having occasionally used the *n*-word—the implication being, *as one does*, or *as one does in the South*—I had avoided her recipes entirely. I didn't want to support her by buying her cookbooks, but I decided it wouldn't hurt to view the recipe online.

Deen dubbed the recipe "Not Yo' Mama's Banana Pudding," the name itself a form of taking, yet here I was, already on the page, a basketful of bananas in my kitchen. The recipe used butter cookies, specifically those cute little Pepperidge Farm chess cookies, instead of vanilla wafers. It sounded easy and creamy and decadent, and on New Year's Eve, I decided the time was right to try it. To make it, you place a layer of cookies on the bottom of the pan, then cover that with a bunch of sliced bananas, then a mixture of instant pudding and sweetened condensed milk and cream cheese and Cool Whip. Finally, you add a layer of cookies, and—voilà!—a chessboard. Then you let the whole thing sit in the refrigerator until the cookies get soft, and, oh, sweet Jesus, it is so gloriously rich, so simple but so good, like the very best things about Appalachia, sweet iced tea and ghost fireflies and steep, winding roads leading nowhere in particular and everywhere all at once, but it is also layered, like being southern in general and Appalachian in particular, like the way "You don't sound like you're from here" is supposed to be a compliment, like the many ways I have tried to wash the Appalachia off me, clipped my vowels and hardened my *g*'s, the way I have given up "cut out the light" and "I dropped that *in* the floor" and "I'm gonna get in the bed" but kept "y'all" and a special knack for softening hard truths. The moment I tasted that pudding, there I was again, church suppers on the lawn with tuna noodle casserole and fried chicken and molded Jell-O salads, a whole spread of desserts, chocolate cake and pound cake and pecan pie and, always, banana pudding.

When I was a teenager, at church we prayed for salvation for the righteous but not for the fifteen-year-old kid who snuck whiskey in a flask into our Bible study meetings, and not for the kids in the area of town where white parents told their white kids not to go, and not for those of us who wanted our brothers in Christ in a decidedly unchristian way, and especially not for the gentle drum major in the band who we all knew was something we couldn't and shouldn't name because he, too, wanted his brothers in Christ in a decidedly unchristian way, and not for the twelve- and thirteen-year-old boys who, during long, dark bus rides home from Presbyterian youth retreats, were forced to play along when our forty-something group leader—a woman with long blond hair and a loud laugh—joined our games, sat on the boys' laps, and French-kissed them each, one by one. *Truth or dare. Truth or dare.* We did not yet know—I did not yet know—that for the rest of our lives, we would wrestle with who we loved and where we loved and how to love a place that did not properly love us back.

So many of us have spent our adult lives searching for a better version of ourselves, of our people, our history. And then came 2016, Trumpism and the rise, once again, of the bigoted South, as if it had ever left. I had had the luxury of believing I could wish it away. "I'm Appalachian but not like that," I had said or felt or tried to believe. "My family isn't racist. My family isn't homophobic." Yet some of them were then and are still, and it feels like a betrayal to say that out loud, but not saying it is a betrayal, too, so I say it here, and in saying it, I hold close the scent of that forest clearing near Cat Gap where nothing but white pines and turkey brush grow, the view of the French Broad from a canoe—dark and mysterious, cool mist rising over the banks, a blue heron silently lighting on branch after branch after branch—my uncle Bill's hound dog standing outside on hind legs, paws on the bedroom windowpane, baying and baying as my uncle's spirit leaves this world, and the sound of my grandmother singing "Go Tell It on the Mountain," her clear a cappella old, old, old as these hills, old as my home.

Replace the milk with whipping cream. Switch out the vanilla wafers for Nilla Wafers for butter cookies. Throw in sweetened condensed milk. Stir it all up. If we just keep tweaking the recipe, we may eventually get it right, call forth what is good, keep what is beautiful, discard what is rotten, redeem our boozy banana mess and make something not entirely new but not old either, and so we shall be born again to live in the newness of the spirit always reaching, always longing for a more perfect home, a better version of the Appalachia that is hard and heartbreaking yet still and always all of ours.

20

IN SYNCH

APPARENTLY, YOU CANNOT wear an Apple Watch in a hot tub. In my defense, the water was not *that* hot, and I had done this two or three times previously with no problem. And, I might add, I didn't hold my hand underwater for any length of time. This particular accident, if you will, came at the end of a weeklong beach vacation and after I had had a couple of beers and was drinking champagne, which is to say that I was feeling more relaxed than usual. Actually, now that I'm saying it, I realize it sounds a bit irresponsible. However, the champagne was in a plastic cup, and there was no policy against alcohol in the hot tub, only against having glasses and bringing your own alcohol, but the poolside bar was closed "due to weather," by which they meant two drops of rain and not what we mean by *weather* where I am from in the mountains.

Anyway, there I was in the hot tub, a little tipsy, a little tired, and it was drizzling and chilly and foggy outside, so perhaps I stayed a bit longer than I meant to, and I may have held my other hand—the one not holding the champagne—under water a bit longer than I realized, but when I got back to my room, the watch worked perfectly fine. However, when I woke in the middle of the night, the watch face was blank. On my phone, I Googled what to do, and Google said I should try charging it, which I did, but the watch was instantly too hot to touch, which seemed unsafe, and as I'm generally a risk-adverse person and, especially, a fire-adverse person, I unplugged everything and decided to deal with it after I returned home the next day.

At home, I explained all this to my husband, and he tried to charge my phone, only to get the same concerning output of heat, so he unplugged everything and declared the watch he had given to me six months before as a birthday/Mother's Day/Easter/Fourth of July gift—not that we typically give Easter or Fourth of July gifts, but we had this year—officially dead. However, since it was still under warranty, I hoped we could get it fixed.

"They're not going to replace it if you damaged it in the hot tub," he said.

"But it says you can wear it in water."

"*Water*," he said. "Not a hot tub."

"It wasn't *that* hot," I said, "and, anyway, obviously we're not telling them I took it in the hot tub. We're telling them I took it in the water."

Not a lie, just not the whole truth. As it turned out, however, no twisting or minimizing of the truth was necessary. Online, I filled out a repair request form saying how the watch was malfunctioning (i.e., not turning on). Then I packed it up and sent it back to Apple, a process made slightly more complicated by the proximity of this incident to the holidays. At the UPS store in town, a line ran down the sidewalk, but when it was finally my turn at the counter, I was relieved to see that the employee was the same guy who had, a few months before, helped me to photocopy a two-hundred-page manuscript and not the guy who had, a few weeks before, helped me mail my stool sample to the cancer-screening company.

Dustin stared at the watch, now in a baggie, then stared at the paperwork I showed him, and while he tried to figure out how to execute the return, I got all sentimental and told him how much I had loved that watch. I loved that I could play my music while I was running without awkwardly carrying my phone. I loved that I could see the time when I woke in the middle of the night to take my thyroid medicine. I loved that I could discreetly check my messages during class or meetings or while I was driving. And somewhere in the midst of this weepiness, I admitted to Dustin that I had taken the watch in the hot tub, a confession Dustin responded to with utmost compassion.

"How were you supposed to know not to do that? They advertise *specifically* that you can take it in the water," he said. "If you can't take it in the hot tub, then they should say that outright."

"*Exactly*," I said. "Thank you. It wasn't even *that* hot." Then, while he was printing a receipt and circling the tracking number, I whispered, "Please don't tell anyone!"

"Oh, I wouldn't," he whispered back. "I don't even know any of these people."

He gestured toward the computer screen, at which point I felt both ridiculous and relieved. Unlike my husband, Dustin could empathize with someone having one drink too many and frying her six-month-old watch in the hot tub, which is what I told my husband when I got home.

"Dustin said he could see how that could happen," I said.

"Who the hell is Dustin?" he asked.

When the watch arrived brand spanking new and fresh as a daisy a week later, I was elated, but when I turned it on and resynced it with my phone, I still couldn't use the cellular data. That required another phone call to a Verizon support person, who was in Arizona by way of Connecticut and who, bless her heart, did her best to help me even though I was not the primary person on the account. That person was my daughter, who happened to be on a girls' weekend away and therefore unavailable to help me log into her/our account.

As luck would have it, my husband was also an authorized user of the account. However, it was early on a Saturday morning, and he was still asleep. We've had this same account for years, I told the woman, and my other watch was on here, but, see, there had been this incident in the hot tub at the beach, and now I needed this new watch to have cell service, and, no, I could not call back later when my husband was awake because I was getting ready to go to the forest to run, and this was the very reason I had gotten the phone to begin with—so that I could make an emergency phone call in case I saw a bear when I was out on the trail.

"Wait," the woman interrupted. "How often does that happen?"

For a moment, I thought I had been busted—for the hot tub, for the omission of truth even though I had never been asked what happened, and then I realized she meant the bears. How often did I see bears on the trail?

"Sometimes," I said. "It happens sometimes."

"What do you do?" she asked. "I've read you're supposed to wave your arms to look big and scream."

"Yes," I said. "But a deep-throated scream, not a high-pitched scream. If you do a high-pitched scream, they'll think you're prey."

"What happens then?" she asked.

I was sitting at my kitchen counter drinking coffee, and except for the power differential at play, the cell-service-less customer and the woman with the cell-service-restoring power, this could have been a conversation between old friends.

"I don't know. I haven't needed to try it."

"That's good."

In between bear questions, she was pulling up screens and typing in numbers. I listened to her tip-tapping, to the snoring of my hounds, who were lounging by the gas fireplace in the next room.

"Look, I really want to help you," she said at last, "and I don't want you to wake up your husband, but I don't want to get into trouble either."

"That's okay," I said. "I'll wake him up."

She protested a couple more times, and it was nice of her to be so concerned about my husband, but, really, he slept like I hear bears do or did before climate change. We could wake him up and get this settled, and he'd be back to sleep in no time and might not even remember the whole conversation. So I woke him and handed him the phone, and after she told him how sorry she was to disturb him, he confirmed that he was indeed married to me. Then I returned downstairs to drink my coffee while the woman typed some more. While she typed, we chatted. She had recently moved from Connecticut to Arizona, she told me.

"Once, I killed a scorpion," she said.

"Oh, wow, wow," I said. "I'm terrified of those. They're way worse than bears."

But she did not think so. You could stomp on a scorpion— squash it or smash it with your shoe or a hard book or a frying pan. A bear was not so easily overpowered. Then again, I pointed out, a bear could not slip into your shoes and surprise you.

"What's the closest you've ever come to one?" she wanted to know.

"A bear?"

"Yes."

"Very close."

The previous summer, I had encountered a massive black bear on the trail, and another time I had come upon a mother and her cubs playing in someone's front yard near school. I assured her that the bears around here were generally docile. "Like giant Labs," I said. I was going to continue, but my account was settled by then. My watch and I were good to go. Still, I was strangely hesitant to end our conversation.

"Well, have a good run," she said.

"Thank you," I said. "You may have saved a life today."

I was exaggerating, but now that we were friends, she got that, and we hung up like old friends often do, still chuckling, amused by our stories about moving cross-country and stamping out scorpions and running down wooded trails with only a scared-of-his-own-shadow hound dog and an Apple Watch standing between you and the next wide-awake black bear, by all the things we had said and all the things we hadn't said, all the ways we were afraid to die and all the ways we kept on living nonetheless.

21

SURPRISEMENT

ONE EVENING, READING a student essay, I came across the phrase "much to my surprisement," which, naturally, surprised me, what with grammar-check and spell-check and all, but the more I thought about it, the more I came to appreciate the writer's intent. After all, *surprise* is akin to *amaze* and *astonish* and *bewilder* and *excite* and *wonder*, all which could be amended with "ment" to indicate not just a transitory sensation or static thing but a whole state of being. Why should surprise be any different? The more I considered it, the more sense it made, and the more sense it made, the more shortsighted my blue-inked circle around the word appeared.

Surprisement, as I saw it, connoted a stronger, more visceral response than simple surprise. For example, a holiday card from an old friend is a nice surprise but not a surprisement. However, a cooler of Jeni's ice cream shipped directly to your front door, given your fondness for ice cream and Jeni's holiday flavors such as eggnog and pistachio macaron and cranberry crumble especially, might, on a day where the internet is out, the water pipe is clogged (*again*), the power company truck is blocking your driveway exactly when you need to leave for work, turn everything around, change your whole attitude, your entire outlook on the human condition, and therefore rise to the level of suprisement. *We're not so doomed after all*, you might think for an hour or two or even a day. *All is not yet lost.*

Of course, not all surprisements are good. Take, for example, wolf spiders, named for their giganticness and furriness, their decidedly wolflikeness. In fact, I would much rather encounter a wolf than a wolf spider in my house. A wolf doesn't carry its babies in a sack on its back like a poached egg. A wolf can't burrow in your boots. A wolf can't appear out of nowhere and cling to your kitchen walls or hide under the ceramic cups in your sink. A wolf can't attach to your body without you even realizing it's there, but a wolf spider can. Once, I picked up a shirt from a pile of laundry. I felt it before I saw it.

"Something's on me," I said, almost to myself.

When I looked down, a massive wolf spider clung to my bare forearm. No, it covered my forearm. Put another way, my forearm was not visible due to the immenseness of this spider. It was so very, very big. Amazonian. I have always had an intense fear of spiders, and in my panic, I screamed, and my daughter, who had the misfortune of being at the wrong place at the wrong time, which is to say right next to me, screamed. I flung the spider across the room, and just before she (the spider) hit the floor, I remembered about the babies. If you swung a broom or stick or whatever at a new mom—I wasn't going to, but *if* you did—her babies could fall off and scatter helter-skelter, the one spider now . . . twenty? Thirty? Terror multiplied. Terror tenfold.

Though that didn't happen, the point was that it *could* have, and for a solid week after that, I slept with the lights on. Then, for weeks and maybe even months afterward, I operated under a state of heightened vigilance. Each morning, I shook out my shirt and inspected it before putting it on. I turned out the sleeves of jackets and the legs of pants. I stuffed socks into my barn boots and tied a plastic bag around the top whenever I took them off. Every night before getting into bed, I lifted the covers, shone the light from my phone into the dark corners under the blankets. The surprisement had sent me into a state of startlement, shockment, maybe even stunment.

At the time, I didn't have the words to fully express my distress, my horror, my complete and total unhingement about the way life can sneak up on you all creepy and crawly, about how one moment you think you are safe, and the next moment you know you are absolutely *not* safe, that you have never been safe from terror, from sorrow, from regret, from all the many ways you might become undone if you are not vigilant. Still, I suppose, considered another way—by which I mean a considerable distance from a real, live wolf spider—even wolf spiders are remarkable in their own way, the way females cart all those babies around even after they've left the egg sack, mothering as mothers do, the way they can sprint a couple of feet per second in search of prey, the way they are too badass for webs and just hang out on the ground or in doorways or in the eaves of your house, mighty eight-eyed, eight-legged fortresses, protecting their own, reminders, perhaps, that even the scariest, hardest things eventually move on, scatter up the walls and leave us breathless for having seen them, our lives forever rearranged. In just this way a certain word you thought you knew can transform all you know or believe you know, and realizing it is so, that nothing remains as it is, is indeed one of life's greatest mysteryments, a pleasurement and true delightment.

22

NAME CALLING

SOME YEARS AGO, I discovered I have an uncanny ability to remember things I associate with specific foods. It's hard to say why this trick works for me, but it has, time and again. Perhaps I am more tuned into food than other people. Perhaps I think about food more. Perhaps I simply *enjoy* it more. Perhaps you say "agnolotti with brown butter and sage," and all my senses engage. I hear it and see it and smell it and taste it and feel it all at once. Thus, it lodges in my memory, filed in the pasta section just after gooey, cheesy skillet lasagna from Rathskeller in Chapel Hill circa 1985 and just before Foster's Market chicken spaghetti circa 1989. However, If I can't recall the food, I come up empty all around.

"Do you remember when we went to see *Misery*?" my husband asked me one day.

"No," I said.

"How can you not remember that? It's that Stephen King movie with Kathy Bates, and we saw it at that theater in West Asheville, and we sat in the fourth row back in the center aisle and . . ."

Mr. Memory. He went on and on, providing intricate details about the movie and the theater, but nothing rang a bell until he said, "And remember afterward we stopped at that seafood place over on Patton Avenue?"

"Oh, yes, yes, yes," I said. "Of course. I had stuffed flounder with hush puppies and slaw, and you had fried shrimp and french fries. Oh, yeah, and Kathy Bates tied up that man and tortured him in her cabin."

Unable to continue, unable to remember why he had brought this up in the first place, David simply stared at me. But, truth be told, this was not unusual.

"Remember the time you left the balcony door open at the apartment in the Bronx in January?" my daughter asked me years after this event allegedly occurred.

I tried to recall, but nothing came to mind until she finally said, "Remember we had that amazing blueberry pound cake from Dean and Deluca?" And then it all came back—the assortment of salads (tuna, egg, marinated vegetables), the hunk of French bread, the wedge of buttery brie, the way we licked the moist, tangy cake from our fingers as we huddled in my brother's tiny kitchen, the oven door propped open for warmth.

I can't remember the exact moment I realized I could use my food memory to my advantage in the classroom, but it came in especially handy one semester when I subbed at a community college for a teacher who was on maternity leave. I covered four classes in the middle of the semester, so I had to quickly learn over a hundred names. The only way I could remember them was if I associated them with food, so on my first day, I asked the students to say their names along with their favorite food. The food had to be specific. They couldn't just say *ice cream*, for example. They had to say *Ben and Jerry's Toffee Coffee Crunch*. And the food couldn't be repeated, so, for example, they could not use Ben and Jerry's Toffee Coffee Crunch since I had just used that.

In the past, this mnemonic device had worked fairly well. That semester, however, somehow, in my mind, the foods became synonymous with the students' names, so I called on Honey Bunches of Oats and Pork Sliders and Chicken Tenders as if these were *actually* their names, a practice I struggled to explain to the regular teacher when she returned to the classroom. And so I retired the practice, put it in my mental "early teaching tricks" folder and filed it away.

But then came the pandemic, then online teaching, then, with our return to the classroom, the masked teaching of masked students, and with my mind distracted and my students disguised, I reinstated the practice. Reinvigorated it. Recalled it. Brought it to a whole new generation of kids with a fresh, alliterative twist. I taught it to Kale

Kayla and Sardine Sam and Mustard Michael, to Beer Bread Bren and Carrot Cake Christina and Enchiladas Elizabeth and Jellybean Jarret. Instantly, I knew their names. Instantly, they knew each other's names. And saying each other's names aloud then, after all we had all been through, felt like a kind of embracing, of holding one another in this new light, a way of saying welcome here, to this new world we must learn to navigate, a way of saying your kale does not take away from my sardines or my mustard. In fact, I see your kale and sardines and mustard, and I, Jennifer, bring to the table some Jeni's jelly donut ice cream. We're all in this together.

And I see you.

And I see you.

And I see you.

23
THE ART OF THE COMPLIMENT SANDWICH

UNLIKE OTHER LITERARY agents, when middle-grade agents reject you, they know how sensitive you tend to be, and they are sensitive to your sensitivity. They sometimes even give you a compliment sandwich, which you might not easily recognize unless, like me, you too once taught at a private high school, and you had to construct narrative feedback for each child's report card, well-considered micro-essays that would then be shared with the kid's donating-lots-of-money-to-the-school parents, resulting in your initiation into the rite of the compliment sandwich, which involves saying one thing you appreciate about Janie, followed by one thing you cannot stand about Janie (although, of course, you don't say it this way), followed by another nice thing about Janie. (This is not to be confused with the hiking sandwich, where the line leader is a piece of bread, and the rear sweeper is another piece of bread, and all the hikers in between are various elements of the sandwich—tuna salad, cheese, spread, lettuce, and so on.) In a compliment sandwich report card, you might say that though Janie asks a lot of good questions during class discussions, she needs to work on not yelling out or standing on her desk, but she certainly is curious, which is a prerequisite for good learning, and you're sure you can accomplish a lot together in the coming months.

In any case, all the middle-grade agents who have rejected my book proposal to create a kids' version of *Flat Broke with Two Goats* written from the perspective of my goat, Willow, have been exceedingly kind and gentle like this, which is to say, extraordinarily good at the compliment sandwich. One agent even wrote with some helpful advice and a note, which in real life is considered basic good etiquette but in the writing business is considered an extraordinarily generous gesture. Unfortunately, he said in his note, because he was not an animal person per se, he didn't feel he was the right person to champion this work. Normally, I would have let feedback like that go, file it safely away in case it might be useful in future queries, but in researching the agent I had discovered he used to work for Sesame Street, and he seemed like a good-humored type, so I wrote back and thanked him for his (narrative) feedback and said I got his point about animal protagonists, but, to be clear, Big Bird was/is, in fact, an animal. He emailed me back a laugh emoji, which was one of the biggest wins I've ever had in all my years of querying manuscripts, almost as big as the day I was actually offered representation from another agent for this manuscript, the one you're currently reading, which is to say I got a smiley face from a guy who used to work for Sesame Street, which was almost as good as a *yes*.

24

BATHROOM TROUBLES

AT THE RANGER station bathroom in the forest, a young girl, maybe five or six years old, paced back and forth. Impatient, I rushed past her into a stall and closed the door. I was on a schedule. Dogs out, coffee, goats out, more coffee, run in the forest, work, bed. Repeat.

"Just pick one," I heard the girl's mother say.

But the pacing continued, tiny Nike-clad feet pacing back and forth past my stall door.

"Pick one," the mother said again, "or I'm going to pick for you."

She sounded serious, and I, for one, believed she *was* serious, but the child was unimpressed, uninspired. She could not choose, and when I came out of the stall, the girl and her mother were gone, which was disappointing now that I felt somewhat invested in the outcome. Not to worry, though. In the parking lot, I easily found them again. The mother stood by the open door of an SUV, a baby on her hip, and though my headphones were on, my music already playing, I could hear the girl's distraught screams. The mother calmly rocked the baby and spoke in soothing tones to either the girl or the infant or maybe both, which did nothing to abate the child's distress. She needed to *pee*. She needed to pee *now*.

And on and on and oh, how I sympathized with that child, who had begun with five available doors, only to find one bathroom out of order and another one occupied, which left her only three doors, none of them perfect, this being a campground, after all, none of them like her bathroom at home, and I could see her fifteen years from now, a long-legged, Nike-clad college student sitting around a campfire with her friends playing "Would You Rather?"—as in, *Would you rather freeze to death or starve to death? Would you rather be eaten by a bear or stomped to death by a lion? Would you rather have a cat or a dog? Would you rather live in the city or the country?*—and I knew for certain that the questions themselves would unsettle her, maybe even haunt her. She was just that kind of kid. I, too, had been that kind of kid, and here I was, all these years later, no better at the "Would You Rather?" game than I had been as a child.

Recently, a student asked me whether I was a cat person or a dog person. I paused, took a good look at the kid. I was pretty sure he was a cat person. A finicky eater. The tidy type. The doesn't-like-to-get-jumped-on-and-muddied type. The enjoys-curling-up-with-a-good-book type. And so I stepped gingerly around the question, murmured something about being a generalist in this area, a lover of all mammals.

The truth is, however, that while I am very fond of my two cats, and there is nothing whatsoever wrong with them except for the fact that they are in no way dogs, this is hard to explain to a cat person without offending them because, and I know I'm generalizing here, cat people can be extraordinarily sensitive. I couldn't have explained, for instance, that I like my two cats because they don't attack me, because they sit in my lap and cuddle with me, because they look cute when they're making little predatorial, throaty sounds at the hummingbirds outside my window. Naming these things seems too specific, too conditional, too reductive (you wouldn't name what you liked about your child, would you?), but the truth is I don't love *love* them like I do my dogs. I don't think about them when I'm not home. I don't think, *Gee, I wish I had brought my cat on this hike.* Or, *Wow, I sure need to bring my cat to this brewery sometime so it can play with all the other cats.*

Perhaps this sounds harsh, but the point I'm trying to make is that asking whether someone prefers cats or dogs strikes me as a perfectly legitimate way of getting to know a person. Are you a hunkering-down-and-cozying-up sort? The sneaking-up-on-you sort? Or are you the boundless-energy, nose-blooping, somewhat clueless, megadose-of-positivity type? Are you sometimes too much for your own good? Though these, too, are generalizations, they quickly get us to the one, most vital question, the one that contains or carries or perhaps conveys or eclipses or circumvents or encompasses all the most vital questions: What is the essence of you? Which is, of course, impossible to answer, so we offer these arbitrary questions as a sort of litmus test to get closer to something true.

A number of years ago, when I taught high school for a few semesters, a student asked whether I was more of a city or a country person. It didn't seem like the usual time-killing, postponing-the-vocabulary-quiz sort of question. Rather, it seemed to come from a place of genuine curiosity, so I tried to genuinely answer. I rambled off all the things I loved about cities: Art museums and parks and coffee shops and restaurants and theaters. The way the air smells of diesel and garlic and curry and lemongrass and, yes, sometimes urine. All the different people, old people, young people, in-between people wearing long coats and closed-toe shoes, no Birkenstocks or Chacos or flip-flops, nothing that would allow their toes to be stepped on or caught in a grate or run over. I said I loved the sound of all those different accents, all the voices rising and falling and rising again over honking horns and idling bus engines, shoes click-clicking past your hotel window, the way you can have any and every type of food delivered to your room five seconds after you order it, the way you could stay in your room all day just being you and no one would notice, or you could walk right out your hotel door, any door, really, and be somewhere and someone with somewhere to be. The very thought of it took my breath, and when I paused, my student, himself a city person, nodded.

"So you're a city person, then?"

No. Not exactly. Or not completely. Or not always. Then I went on and on naming all the things I liked about living in a wooded hollow next to a national forest—long walks in the woods and owls screeching at night and coyotes howling in fall and wild blueberries in summer and the way you can fall asleep listening to absolutely nothing and wake up listening to absolutely nothing, the way you can walk out your door and just be the person you have always been, unremarkable in every way.

"So you're a country person, then?"

I said yes. Yes, sort of. Yes, sometimes. Yes, in a way, but it was so hard to choose. Why could I not be *both* a cat person and a dog person, a city person and a country person, a cuddling-up, boundless-energy person who loves jacked-up lattes and Thai food in bed and the sound of coyotes howling through the pines? Under different circumstances, I might have had a whole other life in the city, a houseful of cats instead of dogs, yet I suppose that in life we get only so many choices, so many "woods-diverged-in-a-yellow-road" moments, and fewer and fewer with each passing year, so perhaps it is best to close your eyes and point—Dogs! Country! First bathroom stall on the left!—then stick to your choice like a hound on a scent, which is not, I might add, a metaphor you could use with cats, which is also to say, I rest my case.

Quod erat demonstrandum.

25

BADASS BIKER WOMEN

EACH SEMESTER, THE students in my Introduction to Creative Writing class begin their fiction pieces by developing characters as Janet Burroway suggests in her craft book *Imaginative Writing*: ____ is a ____-year-old ____ who wants ____. The students then freewrite about their characters for a while before partnering with someone and describing their characters. They then place their characters at a particular intersection in a particular place, where the characters collide. This can be a literal or figurative collision, but the character must encounter an obstacle, and the ensuing conflict must shed light on their characters' deepest yearnings. The characters visit coffee shops and bars, subway trains and airports.

This semester, one student developed a character, a woman, age forty-two, who ran into a younger woman at Chick-fil-A. Internal conflict arose when the older woman noticed, with a rush of envy, the younger woman's long, shiny hair, her smooth skin and slender frame. *Okay*, I thought. *Okay*. But then the next student's story had a similar scenario—a forty-something-year-old woman pining for her youth, the one thing she had had going for her. The next piece had a similar storyline. And the next. And the next. A whole collection of middle-aged women characters with nothing to live for. I wanted to say something—on behalf of all women over forty, I *needed* to say something—but I also worried about sounding too defensive, too pathetic.

Our stories are not tragedies, I wanted to say. *We are not all tragic characters.*

Imagine for a moment, I wanted to say, that a middle-aged woman wants most to read all the poetry she never had time to read before, to hike El Camino de Santiago solo, to receive her wilderness first aid certification, to write a book that wrestles with the complex nature of joy. Perhaps she wants things you cannot, in these early hours of your life, even imagine wanting.

But I didn't say any of those things. Instead, I carefully crafted my words, talked in terms of well-rounded versus flat characters, about giving all characters their due. Finally, one student, a gentle, helpful kid who nodded vigorously at everything I said, God bless him, got my point. When it was his time to tell the class about his character, he was ready.

"My character is a seventy-something-year-old badass biker woman," he said.

A joke. But also a consolation or perhaps even an incantation: May our lives be round and full and flawed. May we seek heartily, crave deeply, wish fervently for all the most wild and worthy things all the rest of our days.

26

TRUTH TELLING

THIS YEAR, AT my annual physical, the nurse updating my electronic medical file did not even look up.

"Have you been feeling hopeless or depressed?" she asked. "Have you lost interest in activities you normally enjoy?"

The truth was, I had in fact been feeling hopeless lately. I had lost interest in some activities I normally enjoyed. Over two years into a global pandemic, I wore a mask during class but not in faculty meetings, in my office but not in the stairway. The rules, even my own rules, were confusing, unsettling. Plus, weren't a lot of things actually hopeless right now? School shootings. Police shootings. *Roe v. Wade* overturned. A burning planet. Didn't any conscious, breathing person feel hopeless? But I was in a hurry to get this annual visit over so I could head home and eat lunch and take my dog out for a walk in the woods, where for a good two hours I might actually not feel as desolate as I did at this very moment.

"No," I answered. "No."

"Good," she said.

This cursory scanning of my emotional and mental state felt performative, superficial, untethered to reality. I appreciated the effort—I did—and perhaps some people were so despondent that they screamed, "Yes! I feel depressed and hopeless! I hate everything I used to love." (And then what happened? Did someone rush in to deliver a vial of hopefulness?) But I would venture to guess that a lot more people responded as I did: They heard a test question, intuited the correct answer, and delivered the expected response. Perhaps instead of a depression screening, it was an empathy screening. Can you figure out what the nurse wants so she can check the correct box and get on with her day? You had a fifty-fifty shot of getting the questions wrong, but then again, the optimists would have a fifty-fifty chance of getting them right.

This work of measuring despair was tricky, but surely there were better questions, more useful ways to gauge the health of a heart. Perhaps we should in fact wrest this task from the hands of medical professionals and trust it instead to poets, who are better equipped to handle such matters. Instead of asking people whether they felt depressed, the poets would ask them: How often do you see glimmers of hope in this otherwise hopeless world? What color are they? What texture and shape and sheen? Recite a poem that obliterates you. Sing a song that makes you shudder. Tell me about a time you fell in love. What does happiness smell like? What sound does it make? How does it ripple on your tongue?

The poets would replace the tiny boxes—*check yes or no*—with long stretches of wide, fertile fields just waiting to be planted. Tell me your truth, they would say. Tell me every little bit of you. Who is it you hope to be? What are your deepest regrets, your fears? Who or what do you most crave?

Tell me.

Tell me.

Tell me.

27

BEST GUESSES

WHEN I FIRST got my Apple Watch, I hadn't yet figured out how to turn off the feature that tells you when to stand and when to move. Every time I sat down to write or read, it told me to stand, which was disconcerting, seeing as how my job involves a lot of sitting.

"It's like having a bad high school guidance counselor," I complained to my daughter. "It sets all these goals for me that I didn't even agree to."

Once, in an Airbnb in Ireland, she and I were sharing a bed, and after a day of touring and hiking and whatnot, maybe twelve miles of walking total, we had just fallen asleep around 1:00 a.m. when my pillow began buzzing, waking us from a dead sleep.

"Is that your fucking watch?" she asked.

And, sure enough, it was. My arm was underneath the pillow, and the whole bed shook. *I needed to stand. It was time to stand! If you stand for just one more minute, you will meet your goal for the day!* Any reasonable person might have left the watch somewhere else at night, but I liked to know the time when I woke during the night, and I liked the flashlight feature in case I needed to get up to pee, which, of course, I did once the watch woke me. Then, amped up from fatigue, I could not fall back asleep.

In addition to the stand feature, there were the move goals and exercise goals. I'm sure the computer had some high-tech way of calculating them, but each time it urged me to check my rings or congratulated me on a job well done, I was right back in my high school guidance counselor's office staring down a brief list of prospective colleges, limited options for a sixteen-year-old who could not do math or chemistry and wanted to graduate a year early. "Damn graduating junior," my peers called me, some of them affectionately, some of them not so much.

The counselor, Mrs. Richards, had short, jet-black hair and wore only neutral tones: brown, black, gray. Sensible colors for a sensible person who gave, I'm sure, the most sensible advice under the circumstances, the circumstances being my abysmally low GPA and SAT math scores, and lack of aptitude and motivation for anything other than boys, partying, and the occasional writing assignment for my high school newspaper, and the advice being to take the first sure thing that came my way. I was, as they say, lacking in prospects, which is what poor Mrs. Richards must have thought when charged with providing me guidance and is what, I imagine, my poor Apple Watch would think if it could actually think. (*Can* it?)

In any case, decades later on the plane on the way home from Ireland, my seatmate, who happened to work in tech, helped me reset my watch so that it didn't tell me when to stand and when to move, which was a tremendous relief and a success all its own, and in the glorious silence that followed, I saw a million possibilities before me. I could get up and wander down the aisles. I could nap or watch movies or order a third glass of champagne. I could sit right there and do absolutely nothing, and no one, least of all my watch, would say a word.

My happiness was, at long last, in my own hands, where it should have been all along. And though it had been almost forty years since I had sat in Mrs. Richards's office waiting to be told what to do with my life, it occurred to me for the very first time that what she gave me back then were not mandates or missives but best guesses based on what she knew, which is in the end all any of us has to give, so now I am saying that I do hereby officially (and retroactively) release her from blame for encouraging me to attend the first college she thought might accept me. Figuring out who I wanted to be and how best to get there, it turns out, was my job, not hers. So here's to Mrs. Richards, and here's to me, and here's to each and every closed achievement ring, hers and mine and yours and ours, to all of us zig-zagging our way along the path to who we were meant to be.

Congratulations, everyone! Very well done indeed.

28

FREE FALLIN'

IN CLASS ONE day, I asked my creative-writing students to make a list of everything they associated with one color, then freewrite about the color before following the prompt wherever it took them. Say, for example, you begin with the color red, and you list tomatoes and cherries and wagons and rubies and so on and so forth until you find yourself writing about blood, which reminds you of the time you were out working on the roof with your dad and you cut your finger, and then suddenly the story becomes about how you and your dad never understood each other very well, the way you've spent your whole life trying to understand him and trying to get him to understand you. Or, say, you begin writing about blue, which reminds you of the night sky, which brings to mind the moon, which somehow catapults you back to a camping trip when you were twelve years old. That night in the woods, you saw a cluster of iridescent blue ghost fireflies, one of nature's most amazing feats, like glowing plankton in the ocean but on land, and in that moment you believed the forest was enchanted.

I gave the class examples, then set my timer. In my own journal, I wrote about the color white. I had been reading books of vignettes or flash prose, Maggie Nelson's *Bluets*, Nick Flynn's *The Reenactments*, Carmen Maria Machado's *In the Dream House*, and I had been thinking a lot about the blank spaces between chapters and poems and essays and vignettes. Rests. Pauses. Interludes. Breathing spaces. Increasingly, I was drawn more to the whiteness than the words, the gap between what we believe to be true and what we wonder, between what we think we know and the unknowable. In that negative space, everything was possible. What came before and what might become stood in equal distance to what was. Samasthiti. Equal standing.

So I began to write. I listed dozens of foods—marshmallows and vanilla ice cream and milk and mozzarella cheese and sour cream and white peaches and popcorn and sugar cubes and salt and flour and so on. Then I moved on to snow and pillows and clouds, and then to concepts such as white privilege and whitewashing and white-collar crimes and white noise, and though it was a rather interesting exercise, nothing cohered.

However, when I asked my students to share what they wrote, one of them, one of those eager, bright students who sits forward in his seat and fills any long, awkward pause with his best-guess answer (always far better than any of my best-guess answers), began with the color purple and ended up somehow with a cello player who was the love of his life, and it was the most spectacular free fall I had ever watched a student do. After he had finished explaining the wild ride that got him from purple to romance, I complimented him thusly: "I loved watching you free fall."

Those were the first words that came to my mind, and, of course, since we were doing free associations, Tom Petty (and Purple Jesus, but I digress here) instantly came to my mind. When my first book, *Flat Broke with Two Goats*, came out, my husband said I was like a young, 1970-Mudcrutch Tom Petty. What he meant by this, I think, is that, though I was already fifty then, like early-career Tom, I was still young in terms of my creative life. It would take time to build a writing career, to discover the best pathways to fulfill my creative visions. Presumably, though, with work and perseverance, I might eventually become more like middle-aged Tom or even late-career Tom—late eighties or early nineties Tom.

"Free Fallin'" was released in 1991, more than two decades after a group of boys from Gainesville, Florida, decided to form a band, a band that landed with a thud only five years and one poorly selling single later. In 1976, Petty left to form the Heartbreakers, and the rest, as they say, is history. Petty cowrote "Free Fallin'" with his creative partner Jeff Lynne for the album *Full Moon Fever* when he was thirty-nine years old. Today, *Rolling Stone Magazine* ranks "Free Fallin'" as one of the five hundred greatest songs of all time, and covers have been done by John Mayer, Stevie Nicks, The Freeloaders, Keith Urban, and many, many others. Though I know nothing about guitars myself, I have read that the song is relatively easy to play, that it only uses a few chords, which is to say it is elegant in its simplicity. Timeless. Masterful. A little black dress in a song.

Petty's life, it seems, was a lot like that too—a trust fall, a free fall, whatever you want to call it. In the 2007 documentary *Runnin' Down a Dream*, Petty describes how, when he was ten years old, his uncle took him to meet Elvis Presley on the set of *Follow That Dream* in Ocala, Florida. And just like that, Petty took one graceful dive off a mountaintop (maybe an airplane is more apt? Or something else very high?) with no parachute, no lifeline, no MBA in his back pocket, no backup plan or health insurance or 401k. He knew then that performing would be his "calling," a term you don't hear very often except in regard to priests and ministers and nuns and the like but which means in my mind that your work aligns with what you most love, with your spirit, if you will.

My student, the free-faller, got it when I complimented the way his mind spun wildly after his heart. Though I wasn't accomplished at the technique myself, I could see so clearly in him the power of letting go. "Yes! That's the way you do it," I told the class. You lose yourself in the thrill of it so that you no longer know which way is up or where you are in relation to the earth. Even when you cannot see the ground, you just do it. You jump. That's how you sing. That's how you write. That's how you live. That's how you learn to fly.

The student smiled appreciatively, but I could see in his eyes that I wasn't telling him anything, just confirming what he already knew, and I saw in that moment that he was not Mudcrutch Tom Petty. In the process of becoming, he was already way past me, his Billboard #7 hit already being covered by superstars, of which he was one, of which I was not yet but still—who knows?—might someday be.

29

GAMBLING

THE SUNDAY AFTER a lovely and lively, family-filled Thanksgiving, just before the last two days of the fall semester, I poured myself a glass of port and was heading to bed to read, to regroup, to recalibrate, when my husband went out to walk our daughter's new puppy down our driveway. Within minutes, he texted me a photo. The image was murky, ghostlike. Something furry. Something cowering.

"I found this Sheltie," he texted. "Can you come help me?"

Getting up to corral a dog that was not ours was not my idea of fun, but when I looked at the photo again, the dog did indeed look distressed. Surrounded by fifty-two wooded acres, our house sat in a deep hollow. Our driveway was almost a mile long, with a wide wooden gate about a half mile in. We rarely had any unannounced visitors, human or otherwise, but occasionally a dog, usually a young, athletic dog, made its way from the neighborhood above us down the steep hill behind our house.

I got up, threw on a flannel shirt and pajama pants. I had just reached the top of the stairs when I met David running up the stairs with our daughter's puppy, a New York city gal who had seen some city craziness but not this particular brand of craziness. He cradled one hand in the other as blood gushed from his palm—down the stairs, down his pants, down his shirtsleeve.

"What happened?"

"She fucking bit me."

The "she" in this scenario was, I supposed, the Sheltie. In the bathroom, he ran his hand under the faucet. Water poured over the four deep puncture wounds in his left hand, red water-blood or blood-water pooling in the drain as he told me what had happened. When he had grabbed the stray dog's collar to look for a tag, she had begun snarling and biting, at which point the leashed puppy had begun growling and lunging, so he had held them apart even while he was being bitten. His injuries in no way thwarted his determination to save the Sheltie. When he had covered his wounds with Band-Aids, blood still oozing from the edges, he headed back outside to check on the dog, who had by then made her way up our driveway and was climbing our waterfall in the dark.

"Do not pick up that dog," I said.

But David loved dogs like no one else I knew, and he was concerned that she would not make it safely up the mountain and that, if she did, she would wander around lost or fall victim to the packs of coyotes that were particularly active this time of year. In our shed, he found a spare dog crate, which he erected in our yard. Then, armed with only a pair of gloves and a towel, he started up the mountain after the dog, now teetering on a rocky ledge about a third of the way up. I watched from the bottom as he navigated the dark hillside.

Moments later, he staggered down the falls carrying the wet, shivering dog. He tucked the dog, who by now was too exhausted to bite, into the crate and covered her with a blanket and the crate with a tarp. While he filled a water bowl, I poured dry dog food into a bowl and topped it with leftover turkey gravy. He opened the crate door and swiftly deposited our peace offerings. We debated bringing her inside, but it was forty-five degrees outside, and she was out of the wind, and we had a houseful of other dogs, so we decided to leave her there until morning, when we would take her to the vet to check for a microchip.

The next morning, the dog seemed fine, but David's hand was swollen and festering, so he headed to urgent care, where the doctor ordered an X-ray and a tetanus shot and prescribed antibiotics. I had class later that day and grading to do before then—grading I had put off until the eleventh hour due to the holidays—so while I tried to work, David loaded the fully revived, snapping, and snarling dog into the backseat of his car. Our three dogs were frantic and manic from all the excitement, all the strange dog smells and the strange dog vibes, and they whined and barked and howled and ran from window to window. Once he had pulled out of the driveway, I let them back outside, and they darted back and forth to all the places the lost dog had been, while I read student papers and wrote things like, *Try for a stronger verb here* or *Try using punctuation here* or *Reconsider this word* or *I'm unclear about the shift in the speaker*, all the while thinking how bad I was at grading poetry, how ridiculous it was to assign a grade to poetry, how I of all people, who had only written poems, and then very badly, back in elementary school or maybe once or twice in high school but never seriously or with any real training, was assigning values to someone else's poems. Was I supposed to be grading on effort? I still wasn't sure, because being a reader of poetry, even a poetry lover, did not make me an expert at poetry any more than having a dog made one an expert dog catcher but here we all were nonetheless.

Finally, I decided to take my hound out for a run in the forest, and when we were on about mile three, David messaged me: "Good news! The dog was microchipped! We found the owner." Noah, the dog, turned out to be a he, not a she. He was eighteen years old, and his home was in the neighborhood just over the ridge. Praise be! The number associated with the chip was no longer valid, but there was an address. Now David could drop off the dog and pick up his prescription, and I could go home and finish working.

Just then, right when things were looking up, David's phone rang. Apparently, when you seek medical treatment for a dog bites in North Carolina (and maybe in other states, too, but I only know North Carolina), the health care provider must report the bite to animal control. The officer on the phone wanted to talk to the vet to confirm that Noah had a current rabies vaccine, which is when we discovered the bad news: The rabies vaccine was overdue—*very* overdue, which meant that Noah would need to be quarantined for ten days. We were to take the dog home, and the officer would come pick up the dog. In the meantime, David was advised to begin a series of rabies shots that would set us back somewhere around $2,500 after insurance.

At home, David returned Noah to the crate, then popped some Advil. He was elevating his furiously red hand when his phone rang. This time, it was Noah's owner, who, having been contacted by the vet, was none too happy about this turn of events, which, honestly, made three of us, four if you counted Noah. In any case, the owner wanted her dog back immediately. Could we meet her somewhere and give him back?

We were dog people. We got it. That was actually why we were in this predicament in the first place. Therefore, David once again donned gloves and transferred the dog from the crate to the back of his car, then headed out to meet the woman and her husband at the local fire department. Did it seem suspicious that they wanted to meet there rather than at their house? Perhaps, but our dogs were all yapping and hollering, and what with the noise and the throbbing hand, he complied and turned the dog over to the visibly annoyed owners.

"I'm glad that's over," I said when he returned home stray-dog-less, and we were able to send our dogs back outside.

Within minutes, however, his phone was ringing. Again. Animal control. Again. Noah's family was not at home. The dog was not at home. Could he describe the owners? Could he describe the vehicle?

"How the hell have I gotten myself into this mess?" he asked me, or himself, or maybe the hounds, who had by then shoved open the front door and were running through the house wagging my students' papers off the counter and grabbing tortilla chips from the bag by his desk.

"What if they come out here after us?" I asked. "What if our dogs wander onto their property, and they shoot them? Did you tell them you didn't call animal control?"

He had, and there was no use being so dramatic. He hadn't told them exactly where we lived. I mean, *close*, but not exactly. And I was so focused on doing what immediately needed to be done that it wasn't until I was standing in front of my class that night, my students' poems somehow—do not ask me how—marked on and marked up and returned, that I began to actually become concerned about rabies. It seemed unlikely. Possible, but unlikely. Still, it wasn't 100 percent out of the question, and it was 100 percent fatal if you contracted it. Also, I discovered from Google, it could live in your system for twenty years or more.

I gave my students a freewriting assignment: *Look at three pieces of writing from this semester. What are the common concerns, common themes, common threads? In other words, what are your obsessions? What addles you? What keeps you up at night?* While they wrote, I scoured the internet for statistics and found an article that claimed that no human in the United States had ever contracted rabies from a dog. Then I texted a friend to ask what she thought, but she didn't know. Finally, I messaged my brother, a doctor.

"What should we do?" I asked.

"$2,500 is a lot of money," he responded.

Always practical (which is, now that I consider it, likely why my brother always had a spare $2,500). He would never have grabbed a strange dog by the neck in the first place. Not on your life. At this point, we did not know whether animal control had found Noah, and mostly we hoped they hadn't. A few years before, we had let our Jack Russell's rabies vaccine lapse by a few weeks, and he had badly bitten me while lunging for a chicken leg. I had told the doctor at CVS who gave me a tetanus shot that I had cut myself on a nail in the barn, but if he had not believed me, if anyone had even hinted at quarantining our dog, I would have whisked him away to stay with friends or family elsewhere for his quarantine period. We would have become fugitives together. Bite or no bite, I had loved him that much. Now, we hoped Noah's owners had done the same and that he was spending his quarantine period being curmudgeonly and formidable and in a warm, safe hideaway.

As for David, the following morning while I was getting ready for work, I walked into the bedroom, and he was lying in bed, his bandaged hand propped in the air like a beacon, his phone in the other hand.

"I'm so sorry this happened to you," I heard a woman croon.

"It's okay," he murmured. "I'm okay."

Who is that? I mouthed.

He waved me away.

Who is that? I repeated.

He pulled the phone away. *The health department,* he mouthed.

"Jesus," I said aloud.

But not without a twinge of guilt. I should have been less annoyed and more sympathetic, more insistent that we fork over a few thousand dollars to guarantee he would not die from rabies. As it was, we ultimately decided not to spring for the vaccines. After all, the odds were in our favor. And so we leaned hard into optimism and statistical probabilities and the beautiful, unquantifiable poetry of it all.

Hell, yeah, Noah, you renegade. *Hell, yeah.* Here's to you, wherever you are. May your remaining days on the lam, may all of our remaining days, be filled with all the best things—wild romps down mountainsides and waterfall rappels and the sweet, sweet taste of freedom.

30

MAKING TACOS

WE WERE ONLY supposed to go a short way. We weren't even calling it a hike, which was strategic on my part. My family members often avoided woodland adventures with me because I could not be trusted to give anyone a realistic assessment of the route length or difficulty. This particular day, I thought we would walk, or hike, a few miles at DuPont State Forest and then head home to eat the skillet lasagna I would make. The ingredients were already neatly arranged on the counter. I did not bring a backpack or water or even a protein bar, just a dog and a harness and a tube of Bobbi Brown lip gloss. In fact, my husband and I had an ongoing debate about what constituted a hike. Was it walking uphill? Walking in the woods? Walking specifically on a trail? What about walking uphill on a wooded gravel road? In general, we had come to agree that hiking, versus walking, implied some degree of difficulty either in terrain or in elevation gain. For me, the ideal hike included a combination of these elements, but for him, the ideal hike was relatively flat—more walk-like, in my opinion, which is why I had to downplay the experience a bit to get him out on the trail in the first place.

On this late afternoon in the fall, the leaves were spectacularly spectacular, a spectacle (see what I did there?) made all the more gorgeous and surreal by the fading light. (The word *spectacle* comes from the Latin word *specere*, meaning "to look," and from *spectaculum*, meaning "a public show"—meaning, look here at this impressive public show!) We parked near Fawn Lake, crossed over the mountain, and at the airstrip took the trail leading to the horse barn. David and Homer, our hound, led the way. About halfway down the mountain,

I saw on the trail in front of me a black snake, maybe four or five feet long. David and Homer were several feet past the snake.

"You two just stepped right over a snake," I said.

David jumped back and pulled the dog close. "Where? Where?"

Since he was the one who routinely dealt with the snakes around and even *in* our house (the week before, one had fallen out of our ceiling directly onto his computer keyboard), I was surprised by his alarm. However, he is color-blind and has difficulty distinguishing between things of similar shades. Like a black snake among dirt and rotting leaves. When I showed him the black snake that was still clearly in the path, he finally saw it. Then, in what I can only guess was a desire to hurry me along since I was hanging back and waiting for the snake to cross the path, he picked up a stick and began to encourage the snake along the way by prodding it with said stick. As one might expect, this caused the snake to coil, and what had heretofore been a harmless black snake minding her own business was now a harmless black snake hissing and ready to strike.

I am not afraid of black snakes, but neither do I want to be struck by one, so I refused to walk past it, and my husband, who had stopped poking the snake, then suggested that I bushwhack around the snake, which I also refused to do since I didn't want to encounter any of the snake's friends or relatives. Thus, my husband and I stood in the trail in a silent standoff over whose fault this was until the snake finally unfurled and slithered off the trail. We did not speak until we hit the clearing at the foot of the mountain. There, David stood quietly facing me, waiting for me to gingerly traverse the gully at the end, waiting for me to offer some sort of explanation or apology or . . . After thirty-two years of marriage, it was still hard to tell exactly what he was thinking.

"You should have left the fucking snake alone," I said.

"You should have fucking told me where it was," he said.

And that was that. The argument thus concluded with neither of us giving an inch, we moved on. We headed down a side trail that led past the stables and down the gravel road and up the hill to Lake Julia, where the leaves reflected in the water, a palindrome. Then we wound around Three Lakes Trail until we reached Lake Dense, then along Pitch Pine Trail and back up Conservation Road and over the airstrip. Finally, we reached our car.

It was dark by then, our car the last vehicle remaining in the parking lot. My watch said we had covered ten and a half miles. On the way home, we talked only about dinner. We were so hungry. We had never been so hungry. The lasagna I had planned for dinner would take too long to make. What about frozen pizza? Frozen pierogies? Fish sticks? Even heating a frozen dinner seemed too time consuming. That left only one viable option, our go-to, in-a-hurry meal: tacos.

At home, still wearing my muddy hiking boots and my sweaty sports bra, I rummaged through the kitchen to find the ingredients. We were out of salsa, chips, tomatoes, and cheese, but we had ground turkey, a taco-seasoning pack, onions, a garlic bulb, a can of chilies, and some hot sauce. That would have to do. I peeled and chopped an onion, then smashed and chopped a couple of garlic cloves. Then I browned the meat and threw everything else in the pan to simmer. As the spicy scent filled the kitchen, my mind wandered back over the afternoon, over last fall and the one before that and the one before that, so many seasons of living, so many arguments or near-arguments, so many walks in the woods, so many rides home down the same mountain. It all took me back to our earliest dating days, when I was sixteen and David was nineteen and living in his grandmother's former home in the part of town that people would later call West Asheville after it became somewhere you might actually choose to go and not somewhere you just happened to be. One afternoon, I skipped school and met David at the house, and though we had planned to cook tacos together, instead we had ended up in bed, and for many, many years after, we referred to sex as "making tacos," a joke we found endlessly amusing. Only now, so many years later, when one of us asked, "Do you want to make tacos?" it generally referred to actually cooking dinner, as it did tonight.

When the tacos were ready, we devoured the whole pan of meat, scraped the sauce from the sides with a spoon and lapped it up, then followed it all with slabs of the Pioneer Woman's Best Chocolate Cake, which I had made before we left and which is indeed an amazing and amazingly easy cake but which we didn't even know about when we were teenagers frolicking around his grandmother's house and *in his grandmother's bed* (I am old enough that just writing that shocks me now), which made me consider how many standoffs we had had in our three decades together, how many conclusions that weren't exactly resolutions yet somehow were, and how glorious it all had been and how glorious it all still was.

31

GOATLY PASSION

I WAS FEEDING my goats cookies, as I do every morning, when our Nigerian Dwarf buck, Merle, slipped past me out the gate and bolted for the does' barnyard. Years ago, when we were still using the milk from our does to make cheese, we mated Merle with our doe Ama. Since that long-ago liaison, however, the does and bucks had been separated by a series of fences. There was the boys' area (aka Buckston Hall, in tribute to Asheville's former Buxton Hall restaurant) and the girls' area. Merle was now in the exterior fence, the foyer, if you will, that separated the two barnyards.

Ignoring my calls and the peanut butter treat in my outstretched hand, he lunged at the girls' fence. He pressed his face against the metal, and Ama, spying him across the field, ran over and did the same, and there they greeted one another with soft grunts and head rubs as if no time had passed, as if they were still in their prime and not here at old age, both of them ten years old, about fifty-three years in human years if the goat-to-human converter chart I Googled is accurate. Though I would like to say that it was only a sweet and tender moment, a chaste and pure reunion, the fact was that Merle was not yet ready to kick back on the front-porch swing, so to speak, and as he dipped his head toward his groin, I could have looked away—I *should* have looked away—yet the evidence of his prowess, of the lust that might have faded into something milder and more age-appropriate but had not, was too astonishing to ignore, so I watched as he sprayed his beard with urine, then rubbed his beard against Ama's bent head, and like the audience member who gasped in horror when I read about this goatly ritual once at a proper book reading complete with wine and cheese and delicate crackers, I was both revolted and a bit encouraged to know that love does not fade as quickly or as easily I had previously imagined.

32

HAYWIRE

THE OTHER MORNING, my barn routine was going swimmingly, business as usual. My Lab mix, Pippi, raced me down the driveway, then romped through the woods while I entered the system of gates intended to keep unwethered bucks from does, chickens from goats, the irritable rooster from me. Leaving the chickens in the small fence outside their coop, I lifted the cover off their feeders, then flung open the door to the goats' barn and began my song: "Hay, hay, mama, said the way you move . . ."

When we first got the goats, I sang to them my version of a Dylan tune—"Hay, Lady, Hay." But now we (the goats and I) were more Zeppelin types, or so I liked to believe. Each morning, they lined up to greet me in the exact same order, three stalls, three families: Merlene, Willow, and Willie; Cindy and Holly; Loretta, Conway, and Ama. Strutting past their stalls, I was the grand marshal of the barn parade, and they were my own little caprine fan club. As I fed each goat a treat, the whole ritual took on a decidedly communion vibe: The Body of Christ, the bread of heaven. The blood of Christ, the cup of salvation.

Except for those days when the driveway was a solid sheet of ice or a snake slithered over my feet as I walked through the tall grass or a dead mouse floated in a water bucket, this was my favorite part of the day. At one time, three dogs accompanied me on the half-mile walk from the house to our pasture and barns, the fog lifting off the field as they raced through the woods sniffing out bunnies and squirrels, the occasional deer. Now, of those original dogs, only Pippi remained, and the younger two were still too wild, too unpredictable to be allowed to run off leash while I did barn chores.

Normally, I kept the treats in my coat pocket, but this particular morning I held the bag in my hand as I let the goats out of their stalls and into the barnyard, and they, upon seeing the treats, went, well, *haywire*. Willie, one of our wethered males, a cross between a Nigerian Dwarf and a Saanen, spied the bag of cookies and rushed me. As we collided, he landed on my left foot, at which point I heard or felt or felt-heard something snap. In a rush of adrenaline, I managed to shove his one-hundred-thirty-ish-pound frame off me. Then I hobbled into the barn and latched the door behind me.

It was immediately clear that I was injured, though *how* injured I wasn't sure. I could not tolerate any weight on my foot. Maybe I could crawl back to the house. Or scream for help. Or perhaps I could hop on my good foot, using the *good* side of my *bad* foot as a rutter. This seemed the best option, and I made my way out of the barn, past the rageful rooster and his flock of feminine devotees, then limp-hopped to the gate, where Pippi waited for me.

For half a mile, she blooped my pocket for the treats she normally got along the route. Finally, we made it back to the house, and though my foot throbbed and walking was excruciating, upon inspection I realized it didn't look bad at all. A little bruised but otherwise A-OK on the surface. Maybe I could shake it off. It was clear I couldn't do my usual afternoon run, but maybe I could manage a walk.

Later that afternoon, convinced that the fresh air would do me good, I headed out, but I could not even make it as far as the car. The pain was now located in my pinkie toe, and one wouldn't think that something so small could be such a big deal, but I could not put any pressure on it, and soon I was all weepy. I told my husband how much I loved October and how much I had been looking forward to getting out and enjoying the fall foliage, and how this was probably peak color weekend, and everything would be all downhill from here. He listened patiently while I *carried on*, as my mother would say, like I was the first person to ever hurt a toe, like not being able to run was the worst possible thing, like there weren't billions of people on the planet right that moment with worse problems, but, of course, as soon as I realized how self-centered I sounded, how ridiculous, I just felt worse, like a petty, self-pitying narcissist. Still, I was stunned by how quickly and completely my body had turned on me.

While I rambled on, my husband, God love him, poured me a glass of bourbon, which was fine medicine, and soon I found myself agreeing that a car ride on the parkway would be a lovely alternative way of viewing the fall foliage. He pulled the car up to the house, and I eased out the door and down the front-porch steps, then hobbled to the passenger door by hanging onto the hood and shimmying around to the passenger-side door.

As we headed up the curvy road leading to the Blue Ridge Parkway, I began to relax. Fall indeed was falling spectacularly, the mountains a sea of reds, oranges, and yellows, the drive itself a journey into the past. *Here is where I ran my parents' car off the road in high school. Here is where we used to go parking. Here is where we watched fireworks on the Fourth of July. Here is where we hiked during the snowstorm. Here is where we watched the sunset. Here is the logjam that happened during the flooding last fall.* At the top of the mountain, by the Cold Mountain overlook, we turned left toward Devil's Courthouse and Graveyard Fields and Black Balsam. As we drove along, we wondered aloud at our good fortune of being born just minutes from here, of living our lives in the midst of such beauty.

By the time we headed down the mountain, the sun was setting, and the color of the leaves shifted in the waning light. The reds were deeper, the yellows more golden, and I was in better spirits—not *good* spirits, exactly, but better. For almost forty years, running had been part of my almost-daily routine, and though I wasn't a fast runner or a long-distance runner, I needed that daily dose of endorphins to feel like myself or perhaps to feel *less* like myself, less angsty and agitated, less afraid of failing, of not being good enough for _____ (fill in the blank with any name, any task). I had run through plenty of injuries before, plantar fasciitis and tendonitis, bursitis, and sciatica. I had run through all kinds of weather, ice storms and snowstorms and, once (accidentally), a hurricane. I had run with a sinus infection and strep throat and the flu. You get the picture. Though in pretty much every other area of my life I was easily dissuaded and distracted, when it came to my daily run, I was, as they say, laser focused.

When I woke the next morning, my foot still throbbing, I was determined to run anyway. I put on my usual running shoes, but I couldn't even walk across the kitchen. The pain was mainly on the top of my foot—near a bone I had previously broken—but it occurred to me that the pressure from the shoe was causing most of the pain. And that's when I had an idea. If I could remove the top of the shoe where it was pressing on my injured foot, I might still be able to run. After some cajoling, my husband agreed to use one of his fancy tools to cut out the left top half of an old Hoka. Then I popped a couple of Advil and headed out to the forest.

Thanks partly to the fact that my foot became partly numb soon after I began, the run was a little painful but not excruciating, and I managed to do most of my usual route. It was ridiculous, of course. I should have just taken time off and allowed my body to heal, but without my daily jaunts up and down the trails, I could not quiet the constant chatter in my mind, the ever-present feeling of unease, the mental listing of all the things I had said and done that I shouldn't have said or done, of all the things I had not said or done but should have.

And so the next morning I did it again. And the next day and the next—for two solid weeks until, despite me, my foot began to improve, and I could wear a closed-toe shoe again. Even then, several weeks passed before I could run at my usual speed. Avoiding roots and rocks, I took special care not to land too hard on the injured foot, and only then, running alone in the woods, my breath ragged, my body drenched with sweat, my hamstrings burning, did I begin to wonder about all the ways we are broken and all the ways we heal and the miraculous way our loved ones carry us again and again and in spite of ourselves.

33

PIE FOR BREAKFAST

IN MY HUMBLE opinion, pie for breakfast is one of life's greatest pleasures, particularly warm pie, particularly warm apple pie in the fall with whipped cream on top. I suppose eating dessert for breakfast could be a way of rebelling against all the "most important meal of the day" rhetoric, but I suspect the reason I enjoy it so is simpler than that, a celebration made all the more decadent by the fact that it is not the yogurt with PB2 powder I have most days and that my Lab observes joyfully, then pleadingly, when I turn up a can of whipped cream and squirt it into her mouth as she tilts back her head *just so*. Sometimes I miss, and the cold cream splats onto her nose or the floor, or sometimes she gets too eager and jumps up and licks the tip of the can, and we laugh at ourselves, at our secret delight, our united front against all that is practical and prudent.

Having pie for breakfast is radical like that. You break all the rules, forget that there are rules. You begin the day with a celebration before you have even done a single thing worth celebrating, unless you count waking up, which I do more and more each day, which reminds me of the way my grandfather amended all his greatest wishes with the phrase "The good Lord willing," as in, "We're going to have a mess of beans this summer, the good Lord willing" or "We'll get some rain this week, the good Lord willing," which also brings to mind my grandfather sitting at the kitchen table each morning, a steaming cup of Maxwell House at his place, the hiss from the cast-iron pan as my grandmother fried sausages, then scrambled eggs in the drippings, which she placed in front of him along with a plate of toasted Sunbeam bread spread with butter and homemade jam. In all the nights

I spent with them, all the mornings I woke to the clip-clapping of my grandmother's slippers on the linoleum, her hair still in curlers, my grandfather's Sears button-down loose over his trousers, the oil heat humming through the register underneath the kitchen floor, the only deviation I ever witnessed from this routine was on mornings after a holiday—Thanksgiving, Christmas, Easter—when there was leftover pie. My grandparents had a June apple tree in their yard, and my grandmother spiced and canned the fruit each summer, so the pies were usually apple, though occasionally pumpkin or chess or buttermilk, and she did not serve the pie instead of breakfast but as dessert—breakfast dessert!—and I would sit at their kitchen table sipping hot chocolate and scraping warm, syrupy apples off my plate while my grandfather sipped coffee and scraped warm, syrupy apples off *his* plate, and neither of us said much of anything at all, so engrossed were we in this sweet celebration of morning.

34

SAND NATIVITIES

EVERY DECEMBER, MY family takes a weeklong vacation at the same Hilton Head Island resort, and each morning I walk or run the same route along the beach, a route carefully planned to allow for a bathroom stop exactly two miles into my run. I discovered the spot accidentally during our first year there when, in the throes of a bathroom emergency, I stumbled upon an outdoor bar and restaurant near the shore.

The problem is that from the beach, everything looks the same. The buildings are all brown, light brown, or in-between brown, which is endlessly confusing, so I have tried to memorize the path that comes just before the larger buildings end and just after a tasteful wooden trash can. From the beach, as soon as you see the building's circular upper-level patio, you turn onto the path, walk past the outdoor showers, then hang a left onto the wraparound porch to get to a public bathroom. *Piece of cake.*

The next problem, however, is finding my way back to the villa. Normally, because my pace varies little, I locate it by gauging the time—twenty-two minutes down the beach, another twenty-two minutes back up, whereupon I search for the Dr. Seuss–looking tree (which is how we all refer to it—"I walked to the Dr. Seuss tree today") and two flags, one American, one British. Then I see the cover to the outdoor bar and the adjacent boardwalks, and I know I'm back. However, if someone puts out a new flag or I forget where exactly the villa is in relation to the tree, I overshoot and end up too far up the beach, or I undershoot and end up at another resort.

Thankfully, this year, just beside the path to our villa, a child, or perhaps a group of children, had built a sandcastle, which, given the holiday season, they festooned with a sprig of holly leaves and berries. Next to this was the top of a palm tree planted in the sand so that it appeared to be a full tree, and in front of that was a palm branch or trunk—I wasn't sure which—but in any case, upon first seeing it, I said to my daughter, "Oh, look—a nativity!"

"Where?" she asked.

"There."

I pointed to the palm tree arrangement and assumed the rest was obvious. However, she did not in fact see Mary in a stable as I did.

"Where do you see Mary?"

The trouble was, I couldn't articulate which part was Mary's head and which part was her body. Of course, it wasn't her *exactly*. It wasn't even necessarily *supposed* to be her. It was more that the whole beachy scene contained or perhaps exuded the *essence* of Mary and Joseph and a stable and so on. It had a nativity-y *vibe* that was very clear to me, and if she didn't see it, well, I couldn't explain it.

In any case, each morning, I ran to the bathroom, then back, and just as I became convinced that I would never find my way to the villa, when all the houses and hotels began to look exactly the same, one beachfront exterior indistinguishable from another, the only unique landmarks the occasional flags—none of them coming close to telling me where I was in relation to where I needed to be—there was the nativity, and I was inexplicably cheered at the thought of the small hands that had created such an intricate display, by the fact, even after our weeklong stay, that it was still intact, unmolested by dogs or sandpipers or other children or even the ocean itself. I picked up my leisurely pace, my jog becoming a run and then a sprint until I reached the finish line, which is to say, the holly berries, and then and only then did I pause to suck in the salty ocean air, to scan the horizon for dolphin fins and pelican wings and ghostly ship sails and all the magic and wonder that is with us now and always, even until the end of time.

35

TRIFLES

MY BROTHER, WHO once studied at Cambridge, has an affinity for all things British but especially trifles, and so upon the occasion of his retirement, I attempted to make him one, not the kind our great-aunt used to make with the cubes of colored Jell-O and Cool Whip and vanilla pudding and pound cake, one both my brother and I remember fondly, but a traditional British trifle, with layers of pastry cream and sherry-laced whipped cream and homemade (but not by me) cake, also doused with sherry. The recipe called for "cream sherry," and thanks to Jacque from the Fresh Market but originally from the French countryside, I ended up with Harvey's solera sherry, which came in a blue bottle with a blue label with white lettering. When the sherry reached the appropriate serving temperature, the word "Harvey's" turned blue, or so the label said.

"How do you even drink sherry?" I asked my daughter, who was participating in this project strictly in an advisory role.

I had never had any by itself, but it seemed, like the trifle, quintessentially English, like something from one of the English detective stories I was so fond of reading. It seemed, in other words, something you should drink when you had a fright, like when you found a dead body with a note tacked to it with a steak knife. In any case, I decided I should sample it to make sure it was good before pouring it on my pastry cream, so after trying some at room temperature, I stuck it in the refrigerator until, just like the label had promised, the letters turned a lovely, soothing, Colorado-sky blue. I then sampled it again, and it tasted no better or worse than before. Mixed with a bunch of cake and whipping cream, I was sure it would be perfect.

Following the recipe, first, I began by heating whole milk in a pan. Then I whisked eggs, sugar, and cornstarch, and stirred some of the warm milk into the mixture to temper the eggs. Then that went back into the pan of milk on the stove. Once that began to thicken, I added butter and vanilla. Then it was time to assemble the trifle. I layered the custard, whipping cream, cake, and fruit (also soaked in sherry), then poured a generous serving of Harvey's over it all, and repeated. I did this until the bowl I had purchased just for this occasion, not a proper trifle bowl but a clear mixing bowl because it was all I could find, was full.

The trifle was beautiful, very authentic, very Great British Baking Show–ish, and when I presented it to my newly retired brother, he was suitably impressed, or at least he appeared to be. It had been almost forty years since we had stood in my paternal grandmother's kitchen surrounded by rowdy, big-boned uncles sporting camo, smelling of woods and campfires, boasting about hound dogs and bear hunting as our weary grandmother, just home from the overnight shift at St. Joseph's Hospital, where she worked as a nurse's aide, chain-smoked in her living room recliner. Outside, cars revved up and down Trammel Avenue. As I watched through the window, the colored lights on the miniature artificial tree turned my reflection red, then green, then blue, little slivers of Jell-O. And when I tasted the retirement trifle I made for my brother, it was, if I may say so, quite good but honestly no better than that trifle of my childhood, maybe not even as good as the one from all those years before, when I was barely taller than the card table piled high with ham and turkey and bear meat and deer meat, all of us packed into a four-room apartment not even a stone's throw from the nearest road, a burly uncle's hand resting on my head, my scalp an armrest, his palm a benediction.

36

RIBBON CANDY

EVERY YEAR, JUST before Christmas, I buy a box of old-timey ribbon candy, that thin, brightly colored hard confection that curls into itself like measuring tape. The very thought of the candies—apple, lemon, raspberry, lime, orange, cinnamon, peppermint, clove—catapults me back to 1975, to lounging on my grandparents' sofa, a candy jar on the coffee table, *The Carol Burnett Show* blasting on the TV, the room dizzyingly warm, my fingers damp and sticky. On the bottom of the jar, the broken pieces melted and ran together, crystallized on the bottom. I tilted the jar sideways, scraped the candy off with my fingernails, the blend of flavors surprising, exhilarating, the way orange became minty, and cinnamon became lemony, and clove became cherry-like, the way everything was all mixed up, nothing the way it was supposed to be.

This year, as I passed my cart through the Fresh Market checkout line, the cashier picked up the box of candy, turned it over in her hands, and admired it, her delight unbridled and familiar.

"You got ribbon candy!" she said.

"I did!"

The cashier looked close to my age, and soon we were talking about how ribbon candy made us feel like kids again, about how it reminded us of our grandmothers and about how often and hard we missed them.

"None of the young people who work here have ever heard of ribbon candy," she said, gesturing vaguely toward the deli. "Every year when we get it in, I get all excited, but none of these younger people have any idea what it is."

"Which flavor was your favorite when you were a kid?" I asked.

"Lemon. What about you?"

"I think it was mint."

As soon as I said it, I could taste that particular mint, though I hadn't actually had any of the candy in a long time. For many years, the ritual of buying it had been enough, the pleasure of remembrance or, perhaps, the remembrance of pleasure. Every Christmas, I had given a box to my grandmother, and now that she was gone, I usually gave some to aunts or uncles. Soon, I supposed, there would be no one left who would appreciate it.

As the cashier and I talked, she scanned my groceries, and in that space, that space where we were both kids with grandparents again, came another memory—a sweet-spicy heat like Red Hots or Atomic Fireballs, only smoother.

"I just remembered how hot the cinnamon was!" I said.

"It was," she agreed. "It sure was."

She had finished bagging my groceries, but no one was in line behind me, so we lingered.

"An older man comes in here once a week and buys up all our cinnamon jelly beans," she said. "He says his grandmother used to give him cinnamon sticks, and they remind him of her."

Sometimes, she stashed a bag for him among the nuts and dried fruit. She leaned in and whispered this last part as if it were a confession, which I suppose it was, and we both teared up, the way strangers who are no longer strangers sometimes do. Isn't it funny, we said, how food takes you back?

Finally, she handed me my bags, and I thanked her, but I was no longer there. I was back in my grandparents' living room in Canton, the paper plant in town rumbling like thunder, the lonesome whistle announcing the end of another shift, a dark-gray cloud rising over the hill, then landing in thick layers of soot on the front-porch steps as a sweet, cinnamony heat seeped into my blood, a red-ribboned flame I could not yet name, because how could I have known all the ways I would grow up and away from that place yet somehow remain firmly planted right there on that same brown-and-cream sofa next to the end table with the black rotary phone, next to the same jar of Pacquin hand cream that had always been there, would always be there, and the same white notepad where my grandfather scrawled the numbers for winning bets on baseball tickets?

When his barber/bookie called, a man I knew only by his nickname, Spider, my grandfather answered, "Yell-ope," then "Uh-huh, un-huh," and "Yep," before replacing the phone on the receiver, no *goodbye*, no *thanks a lot* or *see you later*, just matter-of-fact, his scrawled numbers a stark contrast to the lines in the phone book where my grandmother wrote her sisters' names and numbers next to the numbers for the fire department and the police department, her careful cursive gentle and soft, like her. Later she scratched out the names one by one until only her closest sister, Beatrice, remained, and finally she marked through Beatrice too, a shaky black line inked through her name, my grandmother's fire gone too and at last and for good.

For a long time after my grandparents died, everything was all mixed up. Nothing was the way it was supposed to be. I was not who I remembered myself to be. But walking out of the grocery store and into the parking lot, the winter wind sharp on my cheeks, I recalled how the lid to my grandparents' candy jar would stick, the way you had to squeeze hard and turn at the same time until you could pry the seal loose, and when the top popped open, there it came—that rush of cinnamony lemons and lemony mint and all the good things that could have been lost forever but were now, mercifully, restored still and always, so many sugary, glommed-up, run-together, stuck-to-the-bottom delights, enough sweetness to last a lifetime.

37

THREE DOG MORNINGS

THOUGH I HAVE been running most of my adult life, unlike many other runners' bodies, my body is not naturally well suited for the sport. I am shortish with broad legs and, at times a few too many pounds. I frequently get tendonitis in my ankles or cricks in my knees or sciatica in my hips. To get out of my car, I have to push my foot against the open door for leverage. I sit sideways in chairs and on sofas because if I don't, my limbs go numb. Every year, moving from lying to sitting or sitting to standing gets incrementally more difficult. (One of my friends recently told me that, in preparation for her golden years, she's been practicing moving from sitting on the floor to standing to sitting again, which is something I had never considered I might one day need to practice, but there you go, and here we are.) Still, everything I do now requires more attention.

Each morning, I hobble past the hound that sleeps in the recliner outside our bedroom door, open the doorway that leads downstairs, then grip both sides of the stairway handrail and, in a heave-lunging motion that puts more weight on my arms and less on my knees, I slowly make my way down to our kitchen, my legs not fifty-five-year-old legs but legs like my formerly nimble grandfather had at eighty-five, his lanky frame easing out of the car or recliner, giving his limbs a chance to catch up with his brain or maybe his heart. At the time, I did not recognize this as something old people do, only something my grandfather did, but now that it is something I do or have come to do, I understand it to be an indication of being old or old*er* (but older than who or what?).

When I finally make my way down the stairs, my two other dogs, Homer and Pippi, are awake and panicked. It has been *years* since they have been outside. *Decades.* They may never go out again. It is an atrocity, an insult to humanity or dogdom or whatever. Even though my husband let them out before coming to bed only a couple of hours before, they leap and twirl and whine and scratch frantically at the door while I put on their collars and unlatch the door. They tear outside and up the waterfall to bark at whatever smells the night has left behind—scent of rabbit, scent of deer, maybe even fox or bear. I watch for a moment through the row of windows that line our kitchen wall, then turn to start my coffee.

Not so long ago, my husband and I had seven dogs and three kids at home. Our mornings then were chaotic and wild, sometimes in a good way, sometimes not. Back then, I made drip coffee each morning, sometimes even Keurig coffee—the faster, the better. A couple of years after we moved to this cabin, after our kids were grown and gone, however, I switched to using a French press. I love the ritual, the precision, the wonderful predictability. Making coffee this way is a slow process, one I would never have had the patience for when I was younger, but now my gaze has drawn closer to home, my attention often inward, my focus on smaller, nearby things. I run water into a pot and put it on the stove to heat. Then I grind the coffee beans I buy from a roaster just down the road.

I could easily walk there if a highway didn't cut through our road and theirs. Instead I drive, and that, too, is a ritual now. If I'm on my way home from a run with Homer, he and I order a puppucino from the drive-through. He tosses the cup into the air, and whipped cream flies everywhere as he catches the milk bone inside. If he's not with me, I park and go into the dimly lit store. The coffee names are forest themed, and though I know what kind I want, I head for the bags that line the far wall and smell each one: Ridgeline, named after a popular biking trail at DuPont State Forest. Squirrely Blend, in honor of the white squirrels that live here. Panthertown Punch, named after a back-country hiking area in nearby Nantahala National Forest. And on and on: DuPont Dark, Shining Rock, Balsam Blend, Parkway Pick Me Up. Names and places as familiar to me as my own hands.

When it first opened, my favorite employee at the coffee shop was a teenager I called Lavender because the roaster had to discontinue my favorite latte when she broke out in hives after smelling the lavender syrup. Lavender was usually cheerful and upbeat, if a bit clueless, but once, when I asked for ground coffee, she rolled her eyes and said, "Okay. But we don't have any ground, so I'm going to have to grind it."

"Sure thing," I said.

Another time, I came in wearing a hat and running clothes, and she asked whether I had a sister.

"There's another woman who comes in here who looks just like you," she said.

I'm pretty sure she was confusing the going-to-work me and the been-for-a-run me, but I played along. "Really? You don't say."

Lavender the person, like lavender the latte, however, was eventually discontinued, and the new barista was completely competent, though not as interesting. I didn't even have a nickname for her yet.

This is the sort of thing I consider while, alone in the kitchen waiting for the coffee water to simmer, I listen to Leila Fidel or Steve Inskeep or Rachel Martin or A Martínez on NPR's *Morning Edition*, the sound crackly over the radio we bought back in the nineties. The radio balances on a board my husband wedged in the corner window where the reception is best. If the front-porch light is on, the sound is garbled, but if the light is off and the weather *just so* and the radio turned at just the right angle, it still works perfectly fine. Most days, I leave it on all day, a habit I began when we moved here ten years ago and the isolation of the woods still felt oppressive rather than peaceful. Now, I have grown accustomed to the calm and the quiet, or it has grown accustomed to me. Still, listening to this same station— 88.7 WNCW—over the years has given me a sense that time is standing still or that, perhaps, out here in the woods, another type of time exists.

I fill the French press canister with six scoops of freshly ground coffee, then stare at the water in the pot. It should be almost simmering, but not quite, tiny bubbles gathering at the edges of the pot but nothing too big, a soft hissing sound but not a gurgling. I sense it more than see it, my body carefully tuned to the rise of steam, to the tiniest variation in sound. When the water is ready, I pour it over the beans, stir, and lock the lid in place. Then I open the cabinet and peruse my collection of mugs, another task I approach with rapt attention. Most of my mugs come from the same local pottery shop, and though I have a few favorites, each morning this decision feels new and important. Do I choose the deep-water-blue mug with a handle I can wrap my hand inside, like a glove? Or perhaps the small cream one with a purple rim so the coffee stays warmer longer and the ratio of cream to coffee is greater? Or maybe a medium-sized one that offers the best of both worlds? Once I decide, I measure the cream—exactly one tablespoon, no matter the mug size. I began doing this once years ago when I was counting calories—twenty per tablespoon, two tablespoons per day. Now, I do it mostly out of habit, a certainty I can bring to my day.

While the coffee brews, I let the dogs back in and measure food into their slow-down bowls—two cups for Homer, one and a quarter for Pippi. Homer likes to eat in his crate, Pippi in the dining room. She sits by the pink slow-down bowl, then waits for my command: "Get it!" Each morning, we are delighted anew at the joy of breakfast, at the pleasure of locking eyes for one second, two seconds before I release her. (How do I know this delights her? Some mornings, she sneaks past me, grabs a few bites of food, then backs up and sits when she sees me coming, her eyes bright and mischievous. She chews loudly, obnoxiously, while she waits for me to speak. *Okay, okay. We'll do your game now.*) Then I run upstairs and feed Roo, the other hound, one cup of food she will fiercely guard from the cats until she tires of being a tyrant and decides to eat it. "She needs a speed-up bowl," my husband and I often joke. But she knows that after breakfast, she goes outside, and unlike the other dogs, she was once a stray, so she has learned to appreciate the good life, sleeping in, staying warm, eating a leisurely breakfast.

When the coffee is ready, I know without looking at the clock, though I look anyway. Four minutes exactly. I press down the top, then pour the dark liquid into my mug and sit at the counter sipping my coffee and eating my yogurt, Pippi at my feet, waiting to lick my bowl. Together, we watch the light shimmer through the trees outside. Beyond our side yard is a second waterfall, but we can't see it from here. In fact, I have only been once or twice because it's technically outside our property line. Still, I suspect Pippi has been there many times. Sometimes when I call her and she doesn't come right away, I picture her there, basking in the mist of her own private waterfall, the one I would have to navigate sticks and limbs and mud and brambles to find, the one that has now taken on a somewhat mythological status in my mind, a magical place just out of reach.

In this misty space of morning, I sometimes text my daughter what I dreamed the night before: I was a dog licking water from a bowl. Our goats broke out of their barn and into our house, where one of them peed on the carpet. A Cadillac pulled up in the parking lot next to me, and a scary short-haired Pointer was driving. His elbow was flung out the open window, and I could see his hat on the seat beside him—an old fedora.

"Mom. Seriously?"

"Seriously."

"Are you on 'shrooms?"

"No, honey. I'm just like this. You know that."

Like this in that I have weird dreams, that my high school nickname was DreamWeaver, that that was what my husband called me when I first met him almost forty years ago, like this in that the line between the animal world and the human world is so thin in my waking life that it often disappears entirely in my dreams.

Eventually, I throw on my barn coat, fill my pockets with treats, gather bread and vegetable scraps for our chickens, and head to the barn with Pippi. Homer, who is prone to run up the mountainside, stays inside with Roo until we are done. As Pippi waits by the barn gate, I feed each goat a treat—Nilla Wafers for the picky eaters, Mother Hubbard biscuits for the rest. I let them out of their stalls, then open the door to the chicken yard and dart out before the rooster can charge me. "Jesus, it's just a chicken," my husband says. "You aren't scared of a chicken, are you?" But the chicken hates me in general and my fluffy white L.L. Bean jacket in particular. Apparently, I look like a competitor in it. He has a nasty look about him and even nastier talons, so I slam the gate behind me before he catches me.

At the gate, I reward Pippi for her good behavior. Two treats by the gate, one where the fence ends and the hosta patch begins, one more at the front door. If I don't give them to her right away, she blocks me, drags them from my pocket. Simply walking back is a full-body workout, and by the time I get to the house, my limbs are light and loose, nimble almost. I can navigate the stairs on my own. I hardly need the rail at all.

Then the next morning, it begins again. I wake stiff and sore, aware of every one of my fifty-five years. Still, if I had to say which one I prefer, all the years I was so effortlessly agile or this moment here, my limbs stove up, as my grandmother would say, from years of running, from sitting at my desk typing or, perhaps, just from the accumulation of years because this is what comes to all of us eventually, no matter what we do, no matter how much we want to believe that we will be the exception to the rule, I would hands down choose now, these quiet moments in the kitchen with the morning light seeping in, the air filled with the scent of coffee and woodsmoke, my husband asleep upstairs, the room still warm from the fire he built the night before, the easy companionship of three steadfast dogs and all the ways I discover the world anew each morning.

I am here.

I am here.

I am still here.

38

HEADSHOTS

ONE WARM MARCH morning, I found myself standing slightly on the side of a not-too-busy road behind a concave aluminum device positioned just in such a way as to maximize the right light and minimize the wrong light, to throw me in the best light, in other words. The device somehow simultaneously evoked for me the devices used to protect one's vital organs during dental X-rays and those reflective rafts used for optimizing sun exposure and those shiny things you're supposed to throw on the ground when you're lost in the woods. Wearing black jeans, a black T-shirt, Hokas, the photographer was cheerful, patient, effortlessly cool. She adjusted lights, shifted angles, propped a black umbrella on a pole. As she surveyed the scenery, the lights, my face, repositioned the concave thing, and snapped photos, she did squats and lunges.

This shared photo session was my friend Karen's idea, likely because in my current headshot I was sitting on my front-porch steps, sweaty, no makeup, wearing a T-shirt and ball cap, most of my face obscured by my hound, Homer. My son had snapped the photo just as three-month-old Homer leapt up to lick my face. I loved this photo because my son took it, because Homer was in it, and because it very much captured me at my happiest. However, I figured it was time, past time, even, to update my photo. Plus, Karen had found a photographer who would do the session at her home and allow us to split the cost.

"It'll be more fun if we do it together," she had said.

Which certainly seemed possible, since what I imagined was zero fun. I hated having my picture taken in anything but the most informal setting. I felt goofy, awkward, ridiculous, even. However, having someone share the experience might just make it tolerable. The last clear memory I had of a professional photoshoot was one our family did for the church directory in the seventies. That photographer was like all the others I remembered from my childhood—an awkward, middle-aged man who called me and my mother "darling" and "sweetheart," my father and my brother "buddy," who adjusted the tilt of my chin with a forefinger, my posture with his palm, who compared my father to Mickey Rooney because he was similarly balding. In the church directory, we looked prim and properly posed but completely uninterested and uninteresting, which was another one of my concerns. I didn't want to look uptight, which, mind you, I was. I just didn't want to look that way in my photo.

During our preliminary phone call, Ellie, the photographer, had asked whether I had any areas of my body that I was self-conscious about.

"My neck," I had said.

"I'm right there with you," she had said.

But the moment I saw her, I knew she meant this metaphorically, that she understood my concerns, that she was of the age to *potentially* have a problematic neck, but she did not in fact have one yet. Even though we also discussed what we would wear and even though I had packed half my closet—four blazers, a jean dress, two sweaters, a pair of boots, a pair of clogs, two pairs of jeans—and now two twin beds in Karen's house were filled with my clothes, I had forgotten the shirt I meant to bring to wear under the sweaters. Not to worry, Ellie said. We chose a lightweight pink sweater for me, a beautiful light-blue top for Karen, and off we went through the neighborhood to look for rhododendrons because Karen, who was sensitive to these types of things, thought rhododendrons conveyed the right energy. Or perhaps exuded it. Something like that.

Once I was properly placed behind the concave thing with my chin gutted out like a turtle's to smooth my neck wrinkles, Karen holding an umbrella-ed light on a stick at precisely the right angle, Ellie snapped a series of photos, then called me over to view the results on her camera. The light was nice. My pink sweater was bright and cheery and blended nicely with the green background.

"Is there anything you want to change?" Ellie asked.

"My shoulders," I said. I thought that would be enough said, that she would instantly see what I meant, about the way my shoulders were thin and narrow and, well, weak.

"What about your shoulders?" she asked.

She waited. I waited. It was clear to me that we were making a serious shoulders mistake, but Ellie didn't seem to get it, so I called in Karen for reinforcement.

"Look at my shoulders here."

Karen looked.

"What's the problem?"

"They're too . . ."

"Too what?"

And though my shoulders had been bothering me of late, for the first time, I found myself trying to articulate what precisely I believed was wrong with them. They were my mother's shoulders, my grand-mother's shoulders, my great-grandmother's shoulders. For much of my life, I had been heavier than most of the women in my family, and I had taken up more space in a room, both physically and metaphor-ically. I was more outspoken, more likely to say the wrong thing. As I had gotten older, though, I was shrinking, becoming smaller, both literally and metaphorically. More often than not now, I said the right thing, the proper, expected thing.

Osteoporosis ran strongly in my mother's family. Every female relative I had known on my grandmother's side of the family—my great-grandmother, all my great-aunts—had had it, and now my mother had it. And though I had recently passed a bone-density test with flying colors (thank you, Ben and Jerry's!), in photos that cap-tured me head-on, not from the side, not with a dog licking my face, I felt old and frail, small, weak, insignificant, irrelevant. The words were synonymous in my mind.

There was something about the morning light, the ivy-covered bank, the rock walls, the soon-to-be-budding rhododendron that made me realize how deeply I believed this. I had never said this to anyone before, not even to myself, but as soon as I said it aloud, I knew that there was something flawed in my perception, but the images of all those women in my family bent and broken late in life were hard to shake. When my great-grandmother was young, her shoulders had carried babies and hauled creek water and hoed potatoes. Then, after she turned fifty, she hunched over a little more every year until her spine was at an almost-perfect ninety-degree angle. She had to twist and turn her whole body to look up at me.

My shoulders were also like my great-aunt Bea's, my grandmother's sister, who had once been like me, overweight with a hearty laugh. She was my favorite of my grandmother's four sisters. Her husband, Nathan, worked at the paper mill and gardened and raised bees, and they often went camping and were crazy in love, and she had bright blue eyes and called me honey. In the years before she died, she lost all her words, and she would fix those striking eyes on me and speak in her same, sweet voice, the same, beautiful cadence, her voice rising and falling, a pause for laughter, a nonsense melody. Soon, even the babbling stopped, and she shriveled to almost nothing, her back bent, her powerful presence subdued. Her grandchildren, the grandchildren she had cared for since infancy then teenagers, high on meth, spent all her remaining money, stripped her home of all the metal, cleaned out everything, even the furnace pipes, sold it all. My other great-aunt, Lois, was found dead in her home close to two weeks after she died. Another great-aunt, Edith, my grandmother's oldest sister, wasted away in a nursing home. Shrunken, refusing food, her spine curling toward her toes, in the end her body was a dead moth crumbling between fingertips.

Of course, I didn't say all this to Ellie. Instead, I said I thought the angle for the photograph was bad, that I might look better if I turned to the side. She said *huh* and *well*, not in a mean way, in an I-am-listening-but-not-quite-agreeing way. And then she said, "I think you look powerful." I only half believed her, but she was the expert so I agreed to try it her way.

Later, when I saw the photos, I loved the image Ellie had conjured with all her technical wizardry and artistic know-how, and I began to consider the gift of seeing, something Karen, a spiritualist of sorts, is more acquainted with than I am, the gift of seeing others, but also the gift of reseeing, of reconsidering for a moment what it means to be powerful, like the way my great-aunt Bea loved those grandkids in spite of all they did, the way believing in their essential goodness was her superpower, the way my great-grandmother raised ten babies in a log cabin no bigger than my dining room and kitchen, no running water, no heat, no electricity, just a determination that leaves me breathless every time I try and fail to imagine it. And my grandmother, the way she kept us all together, not just my grandfather and my parents and brother and me and my uncle and aunt and cousin but all of her siblings and their spouses and children and grandchildren, the way her arms were large enough to hold us all, and my mother, the way she took swimming lessons right along with me when I was a kid. I stood on the dock and watched her dive into a murky mountain lake for the very first time. For one, two, three terrible seconds, I thought she was lost to me forever, and when she finally broke the surface, I was so relieved, I cheered. As she swam to the ladder, her suntanned arms pulling dark ripples through the water, she breathed in and out, out and in, and I saw right then and there that if you missed something as a kid, you could still learn it. You could revise the stories you told yourself, the ones about you and the ones about the superhumans who made you *you*, which, now that I think about it, might just be a superpower too.

39

SEAL TALK

IN THE "SPRING" (more on this later) of 2023, I found myself in Seattle for the Association of Writers and Writing Programs conference, the days-long display of bookish vigor and exuberance that attracts thousands of writers each year. Think of it as Burning Man for writers—lots of alcohol-fueled networking and general book giddiness. Generally, I find the sort of cheerfulness and upbeatness and outgoingness required to function at big conferences unsustainable—social interaction overload for an introvert who lives in a cabin in the woods with a very quiet man and a pack of dogs who don't talk much either. I detest the crowds at conferences, the mingling, the polite conversations, and especially all the sitting and paying attention. All the above leave me feeling like I did in fourth grade when, anxious and overwhelmed and, well, crotchety, I hid under my desk at school each day. But that is one of the great gifts of this stage of life. When you are irritable, everyone chalks it up to your age, even if you have been this way since fourth grade.

Despite all of this, I was glad to be there. I had never been to the Pacific Northwest and I had always wanted to go. Plus, I had just published a new book, my second since turning fifty, and the publisher was going to be here. I could meet some people from my press, sign some books, and attend a couple off-site events, including a talk I would give with another writer at the beautiful downtown library. Maybe, just maybe, especially given the bountiful Seattle coffee scene, it would be fun.

I arrived during what I thought was the tail end of a passing afternoon storm—gray, overcast sky, cold, drizzling rain, gusts of wind strong enough to knock you down whenever you turned a street corner.

However, when the rain dragged on into my second, then third day there, it dawned on me that this was not a passing storm but Seattle as usual in March. Back home it was, if not officially, at least practically spring. Daffodils and crocuses were blooming, and I was already halfway through a bottle of Flonase.

"When does it stop raining here?" I asked a local man I met at a brewery reading.

"July," he said.

And wow. Just *wow.* Though I had grown up in a temperate rainforest, I had no idea rain could be this consistent, this persistent, nor did I know that a whole city full of people could be so sturdy, so hearty as to withstand nine months of this dreariness *every single year.* However, on a positive note, never in my life had I seen so many fabulous coffee shops—not in New York or Chicago or Miami, not in Paris or London or Barcelona. There was at least one cafe for every ballroom full of writers, and really, how could one be dejected with such an abundance of good coffee?

Soon I fell into a caffeine routine. I began each day with a quadruple-shot latte followed by a midmorning double-shot cappuccino, followed by a midafternoon double-espresso shot with cream, then a late-afternoon single-shot pick-me-up, and a final, after-dinner, winding-down single shot. Not only was I beautifully buzzing during all my waking hours (which were many, since I never fully adjusted to the time change), I never once had to worry, as I sometimes did at home, that a restaurant or café or bar might have shut down their coffee machines for the day. One morning, a guy stopped me on the street to ask where he could get coffee, and because I had just taken a giant gulp from my to-go cup, I gestured wildly with the other hand, the implication being, *If coffee is what you want, you are in the right place.*

The conference, too, was full of amped-up abundance. Wall-to-wall tables of books covered one floor of the convention center, where booksellers and small-press editors and writing-program recruiters promised to teach aspiring writers all the tricks of the trade that would allow them to publish books so that they could then properly network at the next Association of Writers and Writing Programs conference in order to write and publish another book . . . and, well, it was an *If You Give a Mouse a Cookie* situation.

While the conference raged on, daytime panels on craft and teaching and writing life, literary readings at other venues in the evenings, I often found myself wandering the streets alone. Donning all the warm clothes I had brought—North Face pants, a down skirt, a knit cap, gloves, and three jackets, including a raincoat—I ambled through the market, watched the famous flying-fish vendor toss a salmon over the heads of tourists, sampled Beecher's macaroni and cheese, argued with seagulls trying to snatch curried chicken pierogies from my hand, strolled the Alaskan Way to Olympic Park, watched the sun rising over the Olympic Mountains, took in the famous fountain, the Space Needle, the Ferris wheel, the barges, and the Edgewater Hotel, where in 1964 the Beatles were famously photographed fishing outside a second-story window.

One particularly drizzly, windy morning at Le Panier by the market, I ordered an oat milk latte and an almond croissant. Still wearing my jackets, I stood at the counter lining the window, my umbrella at the ready, pulling apart the flaky, buttery pastry to reveal rich almond filling, still warm. Then I made my way down the hill, through the gum-walled alley to the stairs leading to the waterfront. There I stumbled upon the Seattle Aquarium. I bought a ticket and perused the indoor exhibits before heading outside to see the harbor seals.

Crouched next to a glass enclosure outside, I watched two seals—one light with dark spots, the other slightly lighter with slightly less-dark spots—skim the water surface, then dive to the bottom. Their bodies pressed together, they headed straight for the glass, surfaced next to me, then rotated in unison—a perfectly choreographed dance. According to the plaques near the enclosure, their names were Casey and Hogan. A third seal, Barney, floated upright in the back of the tank, his milky-blue eyes gazing vaguely in my direction. The sign said he was born in 1985, which, I later learned, made him ninety-something in seal years.

Though I shivered and shook against the frigid wind and misting rain, I was transfixed by Casey and Hogan's antics. They were precious, waterlogged groundhogs dipping and diving, touching their noses to the glass, spinning synchronous ribbons of delight. For a while, I had the outdoor seating area to myself. Before long, though, a group of children filled the seats around me, and a microphoned woman wearing an aquarium T-shirt and name tag appeared behind us. For the next ten minutes, she shouted cheerfully over squealing kids and roaring wind while I, crashing what appeared to be maybe a second- or third-grade field trip, hunkered down with the children and listened.

Harbor seals have a thick layer of blubber that helps them stay afloat, we learned. They eat sole, flounder, sculpin, cod, herring, octopus, and squid. They spend most of their lives in one place. Because they are semi-aquatic, they like sandbars and dry, rocky places. Those holes on either side of their heads are ears. And so on—dozens of fascinating facts. When it was time for questions, one boy raised his hand and pointed to Barney.

"Why are that one's eyes so white?" he asked.

"Has anyone else noticed Barney's eyes?" the wildlife educator asked us.

We all nodded vigorously. Yes, we had.

Because Barney had lived here his whole life, she explained, he had been protected from natural predators such as killer whales and sharks and sea lions. He had also received excellent medical care, so he had lived longer than he would have in the wild. Now, he was so old he had cataracts. By her upbeat tone, it was evident we were supposed to be consoled by this fact, maybe even encouraged. But Barney's vacant stare was unsettling.

While the children and I were trying to decide whether living long enough for your eyes to wear out was a good thing, she explained that Barney originally had been trained with sign language. Now that he could no longer see hand signals, he responded to taps on his body. For example, one tap might mean turn over. Two, raise your flippers. Three, lie on your back. He had adjusted, adapted, acclimated to the challenges of old age, and now he lounged in the back of the tank while the young folks frolicked in front.

Even in the moment, the metaphor was not lost on me. I had been teaching writing for almost twenty-five years, and many of my friends who began teaching immediately after college were now retired. At the conference, surrounded by all that youthful optimism, all that literary promise, all those fresh, energetic, passionate teachers embracing new technology, working all sorts of contemporary cultural references into their assignments, I felt old, used up, chewed up and spit out, worn out and worn down, disembodied and disconnected. And don't even get me started on the book fair.

"Walking into that book fair is enough to make you believe there are enough books in the world already," a writer friend said to me later.

"And enough writers," I said.

And it was true. In the presence of so many good writers and good books, it was difficult to believe I had anything left to say that might matter, which was something I had been considering ever since the summer, when I had joined a group of three friends to read and discuss Harvard-trained theologian Stephen Jenkinson's latest book *Come of Age*. This was not the kind of work I typically gravitated toward, but my friend Karen had suggested it, and I love Karen, so the next thing I knew, there I was, reading about philosophy and theology and growing old. However, Karen had neglected to mention that the book was *four hundred pages* long. Four hundred *heady* pages, I might add.

Jenkinson had risen to fame with the publication of his first book, *Die Wise*, a work exploring the problematic relationship Americans have with death and dying, and now he was a much-in-demand speaker. *Come of Age* was not overtly about dying but about embracing elderhood. I didn't exactly consider myself to be an elder (elder than whom? elder than what?), but it turned out that my attitude was exactly the sort Jenkinson found problematic. We don't know how or when to grow old. We don't know how to grow into mentorship. The younger generation doesn't have elders to serve as guides and mentors, nor does it know it needs them. Fair enough. These were excellent points, and I was with Jenkinson on many of them. However, as he railed against hormone-replacement therapy, cosmetic surgeries, ambition, drive, and, oddly enough, painting for pleasure, I, freshly Botoxed and filler-injected and Peloton-ed, was defensive, even angry at points.

Jenkinson's point, I believe, was that young people need the wisdom of elders, that we need to rethink the growth mindsets many of us carry into our elder years and instead consider those years as a time of deepening versus expansion. By age fiftyish (he's fuzzy on the exact date, as he is with other things), we should be moving out of the limelight and into roles that support the younger generation, a position that seemed to disregard the fact that many women reach the peak of their careers later than men, that we are often well into our fifties before we reach our professional goals.

Reading his book, I was left with a sense of duty without joy, of purpose without delight, of longing (not to mention lust) sanctified and sterilized and moralized, which is not to say that Jenkinson shouldn't have his say, not to say that he hasn't had his say and made some excellent points about stepping up when you're needed, about showing up for the ones you love, for the causes you care about, about living with the realization of your mortality always close at hand. To be fair, I only finished the first 250 pages of this book, but it was a good exercise for me, not because I agreed with his methodology or even his conclusions but as a reminder that joy and delight are gifts and we need to talk about, yes, aging and, yes, loss, and, yes, dying but also, yes, above living and laughing and loving as hard and long as we can.

Standing by Barney's enclosure, I considered all of this, my fly-by-the-seat-of-my-pants career path, all the wandering and meandering, the staying home and standing back while my kids were growing up and moving out on their own. In recent years, I had hit the professional ground running, so to speak, tried to make up for time that was not lost or sacrificed but spent joyfully in other endeavors. I was grateful for that life, and now I was grateful for this one—and the one I believed might still be ahead of me, even now.

What sort of life, I wondered, would Barney have chosen if he had been given a choice—a long life or a wild one, a life spent outrunning bears and sea lions and sharks or a life where he never had to even imagine such dangers? And what about now? Was he content to tread water in the back of the tank? Or was he perhaps just biding his time, waiting for the opportunity to make his next big splash? Oh, how I longed to dive into that tank and ask him: "Is there still time to dream something beautiful? Raise one flipper for yes, two for no."

Pat pat.

Tap tap.

Thump thump.

40

THE GUARDIAN OF THE
LADY SLIPPERS

HIKING AT DUPONT State Forest, I turned off the gravel road and skirted the foot of the mountain until I came to a familiar, narrow path. I had found a lady slipper patch here by accident one spring when I was taking a trail break (which, if you don't know, is a metaphor for peeing) and now I waited for their arrival much like, I suppose, some people wait for Easter. There were other lady slippers near here. In fact, there were dozens on the hillside where rangers did a controlled burn a couple of summers ago. Still, this quiet spot, the one few people knew about, was my favorite. One year I had even discovered rare yellow lady slippers here. However, today, just as I was about to head off the main trail, I noticed an old bike tire discarded over a fallen tree trunk.

How odd, I thought. *Someone must have changed a flat tire.*

As soon as I thought it, the tire began to shimmer and shift and ripple. Then it stopped, raised its head, waggled its tongue in my direction—a large black snake. Though I had once been terrified of all snakes, after over a decade of living in a century-old cabin in the woods, of encountering dozens of snakes, both venomous and non-venomous, around (and sometimes even *in*) our house, I had come to a sort of understanding with black snakes. I would notice the magical way their muscular bodies curved through the grass on their way to the creek bed, the way their skin glinted *just so* when they sunned on the rocks, the way they could grip onto a tree limb or a wooden ceiling beam and hang there by their tails, little trapeze artists. I would be grateful for the way they kept mice and rats and venomous snakes at bay. They, in turn, would try not to surprise me—no more falling from the ceiling above my kitchen sink, no more creeping up on me while I was napping outside in the sun, no more coiling up by my barn boots. I would keep my distance, and they would keep theirs. Thankfully, this snake seemed to have gotten the memo. At first, I couldn't tell how big she was, but as she made a U-turn, her head dipping back behind the tree, her sleek body an undulating wave, I realized she was at least five feet long, maybe six. A big gal.

No matter what the calendar said, to me the blooming of lady slipper orchids signaled the true beginning of spring. Each year, as I ran and hiked these trails, I noted first the green shoots. Then taller green shoots. Then hard, oval buds. And then, finally, the delicate blossoms, like the slippers on the soft Barbie doll my daughter had when she was little, the one who wore a pink nightgown and who closed her hard, blue eyes if you pressed a warm washcloth against them. The flowers seemed, and I know this can't be entirely true, like a gift just for me, like something I had earned from my intimacy with this place, from all these years of hiking these same trails at all times of the year in all kinds of conditions.

One day, when I was hiking on a different trail with a group of women I did not know well and a woman asked me whether I had ever seen a yellow lady slipper, I acknowledged that I had. Where? She wanted to know. I told her generally, but she probed for more specifics: Where, exactly? On what trail? Near what log?

I had recently posted on social media about seeing lady slippers, and a woman had commented that if she ever found any, she would dig some up for her home garden. The thought of these rare flowers being dug up and moved from public lands horrified me, so I found myself backtracking, adding a few wrong details—a nonexistent stump, an imagined rhododendron thicket, a contrived fork in the trail—to throw her off the correct path.

I had felt a little guilty, a little selfish, yet watching the black snake slip off the trunk and into the leaves, I could not shake the feeling that this orchid patch was somehow mine, or ours, mine and the snake's, that, by virtue of my having found it while I was peeing one day and her living here, it belonged to me and to the creature I now thought of as a guardian snake who would keep out the hordes of mountain bikers, groups of ten or twenty riders on bikes that cost more than my car, the whoopers and the hollerers and city-dwelling thrill seekers, here for a day or two, who cared not one whit about the wildflowers or the turkeys that roamed the hillside or the grouse that screamed and flopped like a trout on land whenever you got too close to her nest or the family of black coyotes I saw on the airstrip one morning, one mother, five black pups, rising out of the mist and drifting down the bank, like shadows.

I left that day without checking for the orchids, but a few weeks later, at the same spot, I paused and considered going off the trail in search of them. And then I thought of the snake. I liked the *idea* of her, but I was wearing shorts and tennis shoes, and I wasn't too keen on encountering her up close. Plus, it was late in the season, and some of the spring flowers were starting to fade. Also, though pink lady slippers had been abundant in recent years, I hadn't seen any yellow ones since I first saw some here maybe seven years before. Still, it was worth a shot.

Slowing, scanning the ground as I went, I tiptoed into the clearing, and there they were—a single cluster of orchids the softest shade of yellow. Whipped honey. Lemon curd. I knelt next to them, touched their delicate blooms, marveled at my good fortune. I could not see the guardian of the lady slippers, but I knew she was here. This was her territory, her home, her little part of the world to have and to hold, just as it was mine, and she and I were in cahoots. She would never tell, and I would never tell, so enthralled were we by our secret patch, our secret stash of goods.

41

GAME ON

CASH ONLY, a handmade sign taped to a card table said.

The card table was a part of the makeshift checkout area, which was also the basket-choosing area. You lined up here, received instructions, then returned to weigh your berries and pay after you picked them. After choosing a basket, I stood back and waited for the signal, like a race signal, only we weren't racing. At this small family farm, we were all in this together. There were plenty of strawberries for everyone—the children, the people with babies strapped to their backs or chests, the old people, and all of us in between. That was the vibe, anyway. We weren't here to one-up anyone. We were all here to have a good time. The strawberries were secondary. It was like T-ball, or what I imagine T-ball would have been like since I never actually played it.

Generally, I was happy to come in near the end of a race or bring up the rear in a hiking group. I didn't need to chair any committees or win any academic awards. I didn't even care about winning imaginary competitions. At spin class, when it was time to pretend to race the person next to you, I told my partner, "You go ahead. I'll hang back." However, something about the not-race-to-the-strawberries got to me, stoked the competitive spirit I had not felt since cheerleading tryouts in 1976, when I had been desperate to knock out the other nine-year-old upstarts with my lusty lungs and my lickety-splits, so at exactly 8:00 a.m., when the farmer gave the go-ahead, I was in it for the win.

Unlike the other contenders, I chose a row in the middle of the patch then methodically made my way from one plant to the next. Soon my hands were stained red, both from the berries and from blood, the result of repeatedly pricking my fingers on the vines. Gnats circled my head. In the field around me, children screamed, at first joyfully—"Berries! Look at all the berries!"—and then whining—"I can't find any more berries!" A guy picking on the row next to me sighed.

"How's it going?" I asked, all sportsmanlike.

"I'm working at it," he said, indicating his half-full basket.

And because I wanted to be nice, I said, "Well, that's all you can do."

My basket was three-quarters full, and at this point, I knew it was important not to get cocky, not to rush, not to trip over your own feet, sending berries tumbling across the field. It was important to keep your eyes on the prize, not to get distracted by the cool breeze, the handmade quilts hanging on a barn wall next door, the little girl running through the field, her sunglasses three sizes too big for her face, red juice running from her smiling mouth and on to her cream sundress. What that child lacked was focus, and too bad for her. You snooze, you lose. While she stopped to examine a flower on a plant, I "picked out" my row, a phrase I had learned meant picking until there were no strawberries left. Not to worry. My basket was at last full. More than full, almost overflowing.

At the checkout, I waited in the back of the line as the other customers/contestants took their berries to the card table. Each time, the farmer adjusted the price to reflect how many berries each gatherer actually collected. A full basket was $15, but he kept calling out lower numbers. $8. $10. $12.

"I'm sorry the picking was so light today," he told each person. But they were all terrific sports. That's okay, they assured him. They had had a great time and gotten some beautiful berries. They would see him next time. And then it was my turn. As I set my basket on the card table, a few berries threatened to roll off onto the ground, so I steadied them with my palms.

"That'll be $15," the farmer said.

This was, and, I must admit, *is* a huge source of pride for me. A few berries would have been nice to sprinkle on yogurt or over cereal or to make pancakes, but this abundance opened up a whole new world of possibilities. At home, I scoured my recipe books. Did I want cobbler or scones or freezer jam, homemade Pop Tarts or cake or trifle? It was all so tempting. Finally, I settled on a recipe for strawberry tres leches cake I found in a cookbook from Foster's Market in Durham, and something about the way the spring light fell across my kitchen counter as I mixed the batter, the way the scent of strawberries filled the room as the cake baked, took me back to the summer my friend April was dying of cancer, to the time Margaret and I later referred to as "the first time April died."

I had picked a basket of strawberries that morning, too, and when I stopped by April's house to drop some off, I found her lying on the sofa, her feet elevated, her head propped on a stack of pillows. She had vacillated in and out of consciousness for days, and now the windows were thrown open, the room filled with the sound of birdsong and cars rumbling by outside. Margaret sat in the dimly lit room next to her, inexplicably coaching her through the dying process.

"Lie really still," she told April. "And if you see Jesus, just reach up and take his hand."

I sat on the loveseat across from them, and I tried to say that I didn't think this was how dying worked, but whenever I tried to speak, Margaret shushed me as if to say, *Can't you see she's trying to die here?* After a few minutes, April, heavily medicated, opened her eyes and turned to me.

"Margaret is acting strange," she said. "Is someone sick?"

For a moment, no one said anything.

"Yes, someone is," Margaret finally said. "So we have to be quiet."

A little later, April turned to me again.

"Everyone keeps telling me I need to rest, but I really don't see the point, do you?"

"I do not," I said. Which, under the circumstances, I did not. It seemed to me that if you were going to die, you might as well keep doing whatever you wanted to do, and death would come find you. But what did I know?

We were quiet for a while. Then April asked, "Am I dying?"

"Yes," Margaret said. "We're all dying." A correction or, perhaps, a consolation.

April panicked. Her eyes wild, she sat up. Her face was red, her eyes glassy.

"Margaret said I was dying," she said accusingly. *Margaret believes I am dying.* A betrayal. When we clarified that we didn't think she was dying at that moment exactly, she was relieved.

Then, as if someone had pressed a "hold" button, she got up and went into the kitchen to get us all bowls of Haagen-Dazs ice cream topped with the strawberries I had brought.

"Scoot over," I said when she returned to the sofa. She made room for me on one side and Margaret on the other. Though it was scorching outside, she offered us her blanket. We pulled it across our legs, and silently huddling together, we savored the sweet cream and the strawberries still warm from the morning sun. When she was finished eating, she threw back the blanket and, gripping the sofa arm, pulled herself to standing.

"I'm not dying on anyone else's schedule," she said.

And she didn't. For the next six weeks, while she entertained guests on the front porch, went on excursions, and lunched with friends, we regaled her with amusing anecdotes about the time she almost died.

"I'm so sorry I canceled your hair appointment," I told her.

"It's okay," she said. "You didn't know."

"It's a miracle," Margaret said. "We should have a new book of the Bible: the book of April."

Under the circumstances, we should have been cautious in our optimism, but we were so excited to have her back, not quite her old self but close enough, and she was so happy to be back. While Margaret and I Googled "rallying," April went on living. When she developed a blood clot in her groin, she elevated her leg. When she became too unsteady to walk independently, she used a walker. When someone in her cancer support group died, she announced she would be attending the next meeting, and she did. She saw everyone she wanted to see and told each person she loved goodbye in her own way.

"I've seen everyone I wanted to see," she said at last.

And then she began to fade, for real this time.

For a long time after April died, those last days were all I could remember. In the dining room, the table was shoved to the side, and in the space where our We Hate George Bush book club had gathered for so many unlikely discussions—*What was the best way to cook a chicken in an Instant Pot? Who had the hottest dentist? What was a level four orgasm?*—April lay on a twin bed, her eyes fixed on a spot somewhere near the window. As the larger picture of what was happening became too much to take in, I focused on minutiae: The bottle of Dilaudid on the buffet. The pink tinge of the urine in the plastic bag dangling from the bedside. The frilly blouse of the boy in the dark oil painting on the wall. After she died, this scene played over and over in my mind. *Could we have done more? We should have done more.* And on and on, a seemingly endless cycle of sorrow and regret, yet it seems to me now as I read over these pages once again—Do I put a comma here or there? Have I used too many dashes? Was that really how it was, with the birds and the cars outside and the three of us cuddled together there on the sofa eating ice cream?—there was a sweetness even then, even in our grief, as April and Margaret and I clung to one another, to whatever was left of hope, to wherever hope had left us.

And in the years to come, I would choose to remember us there, our game faces on, steady as she goes, the ice cream a balm, the warm berries a sacrament, the closeness a delicious rebellion, a mutiny, a riot.

42

BACKPACK BURRITOS

I WAS AT the top of the airstrip at DuPont State Forest when a family came along—a dad, a mom carrying an infant in a sling, two young children following behind. The youngest child was led by a burrito, which is to say his father extended a burrito at the kid's head level, and every few steps, he paused for the kid to catch up and take a bite, a bait-and-lure technique that would have been remarkable anywhere but especially here, on top of a mountain, with no food truck or restaurant in sight.

As I passed, I said, "That looks good."

"Would you like one?" the father asked.

"Sure," I said. "Who doesn't want a burrito?"

I thought we were kidding, that we were all in on the joke, but the father was earnest and insistent. "Please. They're black bean. They're homemade. We brought extras." He reached into his backpack and produced a bundle of foil, extending a sort of trail hospitality for which I, powerwalking, focused on my workout, on getting to the bottom of the hill and around the bend and up the next hill and to the footpath along the lake to the spot where I would take a trail break and back around and up the hill and over the ridge and to my car, was wholly—or should I say holy?—unprepared. I mean, who could have imagined it, a young man with a wife and three children with a spare burrito and spare space in his backpack and a spare moment for a stranger who may or may not have wanted a snack but was hungry nonetheless for this act of generosity, for the burrito-packing family with the burrito-led kid and the reminder that always, always, we are in this thing together, this dizzying journey up and around and down and back up the mountain, and what might happen if we all always carried a spare burrito in our backpacks. Spare burritos for everyone, I say! Who doesn't want a burrito?

43

THE TROUBLE WITH FIONA

"SOMETHING HAS GOT to be done about Fiona."

I was sitting at a picnic table outside a tiny cafe in Wales, and the voice came from just around the corner. Scooting to the edge of the bench, I saw the woman from whom I had just ordered two chocolate flapjacks and two dark beers. She paced back and forth, hiss-whispering into her cell phone. Across from me, my daughter was engrossed in a Zoom meeting. Trying to be quiet and unobtrusive, I took a bite of my flapjack and a swig of my beer and opened *Hell of a Book* by Jason Mott, but I couldn't focus. The woman's whispering grew even more frantic, and though I could not make out everything she said, I did understand a crisis was afoot. Her tone was low, conspiratorial, and just like that, I was a character in a murder mystery, the unassuming, middle-aged bystander who accidentally learned too much.

What had Fiona done? What should we do? What *could* we do? And who would do it? While my daughter, for all practical purposes, was in her New York City office, I was free to eavesdrop, to imagine all sorts of sordid scenarios. Was it a sex scandal? Was Fiona sleeping with a member of the town council or the school board? Was she a teacher? Was he married? Was he a *she*? For some reason, images of Dolly Parton in *9 to 5* came to mind. Short skirts. High heels. Long, painted nails. Even though it was 2022, this was a *very* small village, a place where illicit romance might still be considered scandalous.

But I was getting ahead of myself. Of course, it might not be a sex scandal at all. What if Fiona's husband had mysteriously disappeared? What if she had poisoned him? Or did Fiona, too, work at the deli? Was she chronically late? Lifting cash from the drawer? Trafficking heroin? Had she poisoned the very flapjacks we were now eating? Each scenario seemed equally likely, and the more I considered it, the more possibilities I saw. Was the woman on the phone really all that she seemed? Back at the counter, she had seemed friendly, benign, trustworthy, even. But now, her tone was sinister. What if she wanted Fiona taken out before it was too late . . . but too late for *what*?

My daughter's meeting went on and on, and I grew increasingly uneasy. For one, *Hell of a Book* was itself a bit eerie. Plus the morning was dreary, overcast, *creepy*, even. This seemed the perfect day, the perfect setting, for something dramatic, maybe even sinister, to happen. For the past week, we had been cruising down the canal at a steady clip of one to two miles per hour on a luxurious narrowboat with my brother and brother-in-law. The boat had a full kitchen, two bathrooms, a television, a chaise lounge, Scotch in a crystal decanter, gourmet chocolates, potted plants on the bow, and a brass pin for the tiller (a pin that was stolen one night while we slept—very suspicious!). Still, a murder happening in this idyllic place, full of herds of sheep and lush hillsides and fields of wildflowers, was not unimaginable.

This trip to Brecon National Park was the trip of a lifetime, the boat ride a gift from my brother, who had planned this for his birthday in May of 2020, but the pandemic had forced us to cancel and reschedule twice. Now, two birthdays and several cases of COVID among us later, our arrival here seemed like a small miracle. The historic canal, completed around 1800, meandered through pastures and woods and wide meadows, one stunningly beautiful view followed by another. During the day, we cruised the canal, walked along the towpath, stopped at little villages along the way to shop or eat or grab a drink. In the evenings, we drank Prosecco and ate Welsh cheese with Branston pickle relish on brown bread and Bakewell tarts. As we ate, we watched the sun set over the meadows, ducklings circle the boat. At every point, as far as we could see, on either side of the canal, sheep grazed and slept and nursed and romped. Every few seconds, a lamb cried out for its mother, and every few seconds, hundreds of mothers, a chorus of mothers, responded. *I'm here. You are safe.*

However, despite the idyllic surroundings, the remoteness of it all, the not-exactly-hidden dangers seemed to make it the perfect setting for a tasteful murder mystery, nothing too grim and grisly, mind you—a polite and understated killing, which is to say, a very British sort of crime: Arsenic. Sleeping pills and a pillow pressed firmly over the face. An "accidental" gas leak. A gentle push overboard into the lock at just the right moment. After all, there were some real things to fear out here: A rusty control thingy in the lock gate. Rushing water thrusting your boat onto the cill. The pub where we had eaten lunch only later to discover that it had a zero sanitation rating. Weil's disease, or leptospirosis, which, according to one lock volunteer, was found in the water due to the high population of rats. My point is that while cruising along the canal in a narrowboat seemed like a relatively low-risk activity, there were some horrific ways to die out here, so it didn't seem inconceivable that Fiona could fall victim to one of them.

Over the past few days, we had been repeatedly shown, by volunteers and by other boaters, how to navigate the two-hundred-plus-year-old locks, and over the past few days, at each of the five locks we were traversing, we had repeatedly forgotten how to do it. Or, rather, we had forgotten the precise order each time, which was the most important part aside from remembering to keep the boat off the cills. If you got the order wrong, your boat could be submerged in rushing water in a matter of seconds. At each lock, my brother drove the boat in, my brother-in-law stayed on as co-captain, and my daughter and I jumped out to do the legwork of opening and closing the lock. On the instructional video we had watched (okay, *skimmed*) before we left home, it had all looked extremely easy—so very *doable*—but on the way to the boat dock, the cab driver had regaled us with a story of a woman whose finger was hacked off by one of the ancient handles, which only added to my sense of unease.

Now, the woman at the café became more insistent, more agitated, but I still only caught a few words of her conversation. "Fiona," she kept saying. Something about Fiona. I motioned frantically to my daughter: *Mute yourself. Turn off your camera.* But she shifted in her seat so that I was firmly out of her view. By the time she finally closed her laptop and looked up at me, the woman had finished the call and gone back inside. I threw up my hands in exasperation.

"What the hell is wrong with you?" my daughter asked.

Which was the problem with our new remote-working world. One of you could be Agatha Raisin in a remote village in Wales, and the other one of you could be an employment specialist at a meeting in Times Square, and it was hard to fully convey the weird time-travel disconnect you experienced when you both landed back on a bench wiping chocolate crumbs from your lips. Nonetheless, I did my best to convey what I had heard, and she agreed that it was intriguing. We tossed out a few theories and even considered asking our one friend—a lock volunteer who was on the town council—whether he knew anything about the situation. However, it was our second-to-last day on the canal, so we would likely never know what happened to Fiona or why she had caused such a stir.

That night, as I lay in bed that night conjuring Fiona, I saw a young woman, red hair pulled back in a ponytail, fair-skinned, medium height, a bit on the heavy side, a long, loose, pale-blue dress, sensible shoes, a gold necklace with the letter F . . . no, a locket she rubbed with her thumb and forefinger whenever she was nervous, which she was often, of course, since all the trouble at the café . . .

I fell asleep with the soft scent of lilacs in air, and when I woke at daybreak to the baaing of sheep and the quacking of ducks and the distant sound of a boat motor, Fiona was as real to me as anyone I knew in real life, and I knew without a doubt that whatever trouble she was in, I was on her side. I had her back. I would be her ride-or-die, her mother sheep, her narrowboat copilot for as long as she needed me, for as long as she was down and out, which she so clearly was or was soon going to be, which I so often had been and would be again, as we all have been, and as we all will be.

44

DO NOT GIVE NOTICE YET

MY DAUGHTER, WHO has been applying for jobs for over a year, recently received three offers in a week. *Sort of.* Salaries were negotiated. Terms were agreed to. And then, even though an offer had been made, not officially in a contract but in writing via email, which seemed final*ish*, the *final* final approval process began, which, because these were government jobs, involved extensive background checks.

"Don't give notice yet," the prospective employers said three times, as if this were a fairy tale, three warnings in seven days, all manner of magical numbers and mystical processes at play. Or perhaps they were only mysterious to me because I have never been very career minded and do not have much experience in applying for, much less *getting*, jobs. And though this happened to her (my daughter), not to me, since the pandemic, the space between us has sometimes felt not like space at all, more like a heartbeat, a breath, and I, always restless, always thinking one step ahead, of leaving where I am, this job or this way of life, trading it all in for a new, improved version of me, took this instruction under consideration also.

"I'm not too old to start a new career, am I?" I asked my husband.

I had asked him this a dozen times before over the past few decades, and each time he had reassured me that I was not too old. However, at age forty-seven, with one master's degree completed, I had gone back to graduate school to get a second master's degree, the one that had landed me the university lecturer job I currently had. We were still making payments on those student loans, so when he answered, he did it not impatiently, as he might have ten or twenty years ago, but honestly, realistically, with resignation: "I'm afraid you might be."

Okay. Fair enough. But hear me out. Maybe I could try sell-
ing real estate if only there weren't so much math involved, or maybe
I would take a sommelier course—I'd always wanted to try that—if
only it didn't require so much memorization or, then again, maybe I
could teach fitness classes for older adults or lead hiking excursions,
but my knees were pretty shot from years of running, so maybe I could
lead writing retreats in Europe or—how about this—*wine and writing
retreats* led by a full-fledged sommelier—no wait, how about a *wine
and hiking and writing retreat* or—I've got it—how about a *Camino
writing/wine tour*? David—God love him—shook his head mourn-
fully, but I was not discouraged. Maybe my ideas needed tweaking,
but I was confident I would soon land upon the right next thing.

In any case, *Don't give notice yet*, considered in one way, felt akin
to *Don't quit your day job*, which felt a lot like don't get your hopes up,
like don't get too invested, like you might as well give up, throw in the
towel, hang things up, and throw up your hands, which is to say, admit
defeat. But I was one to get invested, to hope too soon, which, truth be
told, was what had gotten me this far. After all, you only needed one
yes—*yes* to this book idea, *yes* to this project, *yes* to you can take this class
on Spanish wine—and pretty soon it was all happening, the things you
dreamed about when you were just a kid swinging on the rope your
dad hung for you on an oak tree branch overhanging the creek, your
legs pumping wildly, light filtering through the pines, the creek bed
glistening below. What if this moment was like that moment? What if
you took one deep breath, closed your eyes, and jumped—landed in
a pile of leaves, miraculously, on your feet? Considered this way, *Don't
give notice yet* could become a rallying call, perhaps even a challenge, a
summons, a double-dog dare to swing higher, leap more boldly: You
think you've seen the last of me? Well, don't count me out. Do not give
up on me. Do not give notice yet.

45

SACRED SPACES

IN THE DENTAL chair, I was tilted back so far as to almost be upside down, an astronaut in training, my mouth numb from two shots—double numb—when my dentist said to me, "Thank you for letting us enter your sacred space."

At first, I thought I had misheard or that it was a strange joke, but when I looked up, I saw clearly in his face—the part of it I could see above his mask—that he was completely sincere, though sincere in what way I wasn't sure. It took me a moment to realize that by *sacred space* he meant my mouth, and my immediate reaction—the one I had inside my head but not out loud because of the aforementioned numbness and because here, in my fifth decade on earth, I was learning to think before I spoke—was that this was most certainly *not* my sacred space.

And then there was the confusing reference to "us," by which, I supposed, he was including his assistant, who in that moment was suctioning spit from my cheek wall, who might in fact have been suctioning my entire cheek into that tiny tube while I watched from afar, from upside down and deep beneath or above or behind my sacred space. The dentist was in his late thirties or maybe early forties, with jet-black hair and bright blue eyes. He was dressed in a way that one might describe as snappy, but whether it was Bible-y snappy or hipster-y snappy I couldn't have said. A thin tie, a few splashes of pink and green, slim-fitting slacks. Moments earlier, he had been prying off one of my old crowns—drilling, then prying, then drilling some more—after which I had definitely felt a bit manhandled but alluding to a violation or intimacy or . . . what exactly was he alluding to? . . . felt like an overstatement and also, well, odd, but odd in what way? A New Age-y, feel-all-the-good-vibes sort of way? Was he stoned? Was *I* stoned?

The appointment, which included two same-day crowns, lasted four hours, so I had ample time to contemplate this, but later I told my husband and adult children this story, and they all Googled a photo of the dentist, and as soon as they saw him, they were like, "Oh, oh, oh. He's Mormon," which is, apparently, a healthy, wholesome look I am not good at detecting, but since the dentist had put the idea in my head (and/or my mouth), I went home and researched the origins of the word *sacred*.

From the old verb *sacren*, meaning to make holy, and the old French *sacrer*, to consecrate or anoint, the word *sacred* means hallowed, consecrated, or made holy due to a close relationship or association with the divine—like a sacred cow, for example, which brings to mind the exclamation *Holy cow!* and its cousins, *Holy moly!* and *Holy crap!* and the like—expressions of amazement, which also leads me to wonder, what if the dentist was right?

What if my mouth *is* holy? No. What if it is *capable* of holiness? I don't mean what if I suddenly stopped cursing and drinking gin and eating too much ice cream. I mean, what if I considered for a moment the power I have, that we all have, to inspire astonishment, to offer solace and encouragement and inspiration, and what if I chose that more often than I chose to be fearful or discouraged or disappointed? I suppose then I might move in this world a little differently, and that I am even considering this possibility—the notion that my mouth might serve as a vehicle for the divine or a pathway toward the divine or a reflection of the divine—comes to me as a tremendous *suprise-ment*, and saying that word once again here so many days and weeks after my student first schooled me on it just goes to show you how potent our words can be, which is to say how sacred our mouths must be. *Holy. Cow.*

46

MAGICAL SPRING

THE DRIVE FROM Shannon to nearby Burren National Park, like all the other drives we had taken through Ireland, took longer than expected, the road narrowing into almost a single lane as we dodged rock walls and oncoming traffic in our rental car. After several winding miles, we finally came to a small parking lot, and our GPS indicated we had arrived.

We had read that the park had over thirty-five hundred acres of limestone, shrubs, woodlands, cliffs, wetlands, semipermanent lakes, and so on. At times, *allegedly*, it was bustling with people and activity, but on that early spring evening, only a couple other cars remained. As we parked and got out, we realized the setting was more noteworthy for what it *wasn't* than what it *was*. The landscape was eerie, silent, desolate, as if we had been teleported from the town bustling with hordes of exuberant hurling fans (hurling being, as I understand it, a Gaelic sport somewhat similar to football) and dropped on another planet. In the surrounding valley, shrubs covered the fields, but just beyond that, mounds of whitish-gray or grayish-white limestone spilled like glaciers across the hillsides. The starkness of the land brought to mind the Badlands of South Dakota, where prairie dogs are as abundant as the white squirrels in my hometown, which is to say they are everywhere.

The air was cooler here than it had been in town, and the wind had a bite that was not exactly spring-like despite the fact that it was early June. Pulling on our jackets, we studied the trail map by the side of the road and decided to begin with Knockaunroe Turlough. The flat path meandered for a mile or so through meadows and over rock before looping back to the parking lot. It was pretty but hardly the adventure we had been seeking.

If we wanted to see the large sheaths of limestone up close, we needed to take the longer trail on the other side of the parking lot. However, the sky looked dark. A storm? Dusk? Maybe both. We had thought we had left with plenty of daylight to spare, but now it seemed like we were cutting it close.

Still, it was our last night, our last grand adventure of a two-week trip. In two more days, my daughter would be back working in New York, and I would be back teaching in North Carolina. I didn't know when I would see her again. Perhaps that was dramatic. We would likely see each other in a few months, but we weren't leaving together, and after months living together during the pandemic, months where it had seemed as if no time had passed at all, as if she were a child again and I was twenty-five, and things might always be just so, the two of us indefinitely hanging out doing mother-daughter things like running in the forest and eating ice cream and watching movies, this woman-child of mine now had a new job and a new life of her own. And rightly so. And praise be for her joy. And praise be for all the joy she had brought me. And oh, my heart. All of that all at once.

Finally, in the spirit of wringing the last bit of light out of our trip, we decided to take Slieve Carran, the two-and-a-half-kilometer trail that looped through open limestone pavement before passing through woods of oak, ash, and hazel. This route, we had read, included a holy well that had been the site of pilgrimages since St. Colman MacDuagh had established a hermitage here in the seventh century. I wasn't sure what a holy well entailed, but I was curious, and I wanted to see the limestone up close. Plus, we could always turn back if we thought we couldn't do the whole trail before dark.

Heading out on the gravel road, we followed the signs until the road became a dirt path, then a dense thicket. Finally, we emerged on a wide sheath of limestone. Frommer's guide to the park had described the limestone as "a kind of moonscape." Sure enough, the rock resembled the moon with its pockmarked surface, only here, grass and wildflowers grew in the dips and crevices. As we silently explored, the thick gray clouds that had been skirting the sky moved in, coloring the world gray—the ground below us, the sky above. It was spectacularly beautiful, but the beauty was stark and strange and oddly unsettling. We had also read that Burren was home to weasels, ermine, badgers, and birds, but we saw nothing from here—no cars, no people, no signs of other life whatsoever. Wind whipped our hair as we leapt over the holes and surveyed the empty fields below.

"Maybe we should turn back," I said.

"Maybe," my daughter agreed.

"It's a little creepy, don't you think?"

"It is. And so, so beautiful."

And so we stayed longer, drinking in the rising mist, the surreal otherworldliness. Then, leaping over the crevices, we made our way off the rock and back onto the trail, where the scenery looked more like planet earth, and the wind calmed to a gentle breeze, and our previous apprehension began to seem silly.

"Let's go a little further," one of us said.

So we set off in search of the holy well. Soon we found ourselves standing by a sign marking the path. Next to it a wooden box was labeled *Take a coin. Leave a coin.* As if we had walked into a fairy tale. It seemed both odd and perfectly fitting. I wasn't sure about the point of the coins—to count visitors? An act of faith or goodwill? —but neither of us had any money, so we turned down the path without whatever protection the coins might have afforded us. Just when I was wondering aloud how we would know when we got to the sacred site, we came to a clearing. There, the faintest trickle of water beneath the earth belied the presence of a water source, but there was no visible spring, which, I supposed, was the thing that made it holy. Just beyond us, a rustling in the trees alerted us to a cow, its thick Oreo flank brushing against tree bark as it ambled away. The whole scene brought to mind *Into the Woods* and Jack and the Beanstalk. A magical cow. A magical forest. A magical elixir.

The woods were cast in the surreal glow of twilight, and to our left, above the spring basin, rows of prayer flags swayed between the trees. A drinking ladle hung from a hook on one tree trunk, and mementos lined the rocks by the water: hair ties, newspaper clippings, crucifixes, and dozens of wrinkled and yellowed photos—babies in christening gowns, young women in wedding gowns, young men in army uniforms, old men and old women standing on beaches or in fields or on city sidewalks. So much loss. So much grief, the kind you gathered up and carried with you for a lifetime, a sight that brought to mind Cheryl Strayed's "The Love of My Life." In the essay, originally published in *The Sun* and the basis for the bestselling memoir *Wild*, Strayed challenges what she calls America's "democracy of grief"—the notion that all grief is the same, all losses equal.

"Imagine if there were a boat upon which you could put only four people, and everyone else known and beloved to you would then cease to exist," she says. "Who would you put on that boat? It would be painful, but how quickly you would decide: *You and you and you and you, get in. The rest of you, goodbye.*"

When my friend April was dying of ovarian cancer a few years before, I had recalled Strayed's words wrong, or perhaps I remembered them the way I needed to, a way that was not incorrect, only inaccurate. In my recollection, eight people boarded the hypothetical boat. Limiting the number to eight was tough but doable, unpleasant but survivable. However, when I went back and reread the passage, I was shocked to find the number of people allotted was not eight but half of eight: four. At once, my answer was both clear and devastating. On my boat, I would only be able to take my husband and my three children.

Strayed was right. All grief was not the same. All love was not the same. Still, since it was a hypothetical situation, as April got sicker and sicker, I bargained hypothetically. Say, for example, my husband got to choose four people as well, and he had already chosen our children. Could I then bring my parents, my brother and brother-in-law, or perhaps my children's loved ones? Then again, what if my three children had already chosen their partners, their uncles, and their grandparents? Could I then choose four people who were not my family? Could I then choose my friends? Could I then choose April?

This is how unreasonable my reasoning went. I needed to find a loophole in the hypothetical natural order, a scenario in which I could save April. Thinking this way, I knew, was a sign that my brain was misfiring, that I was losing touch with reality. And yet, much like Joan Didion describes in *The Year of Magical Thinking*, my irrational thoughts persisted. And later, after April was gone, I was left with only this: despite all my bargaining and pleading and negotiating, my boat had not been big enough to save her.

There in the woods, April's death was not the only one I carried with me, but it was the freshest, the most vivid in that moment as I imagined all the other grieving souls who had made this pilgrimage with photos peeled from wallets or Bibles or frames, carried over oceans and mountains and valleys and skies and placed here as a tribute, a memorial, yes, but also a pathway back through the desolate moonscape to the land of the living.

"You don't honor the dead by burying the living," a friend once told me.

Perhaps the people who brought these photos had heard this too. Perhaps they had learned how to hold their sorrow close and let it go all at once, to move through the world forever changed but not undone by grief. Perhaps they had left their heaviest sorrow here at a holy well in a spooky and mystical forest. Perhaps that was ultimately what was asked of all of us, to keep living in spite of it all, to keep moving toward joy even still, even so.

"What's it going to be like to die?" April had asked her friends once. "We don't know," we had said. "You will have to tell us."

A few days later, at the very end, she said, "It's so sparkly. I didn't know it would be so sparkly."

Joy, amazement, sorrow, and wonder all converged in April's final days, just like they did here, just like they do now, one continual loop, world without end. Now, in the forest, the only sound was dripping water, and the light grew stranger by the minute—gold and glowing, deepening even as it dimmed. Regardless of the time on my watch, soon it would be nightfall, and my daughter and I would rush back down the gravel road with darkness pressing in on us, tumbleweeds rolling through the air. For now, though, we were still in the grove, still protected by spectral cows and mysterious springs. Here, where the line between the dead and the living was oh, so very thin, it was possible to keep your loved ones safe, to hold them close even as they were leaving, even after they were gone. This place was—I felt it in my bones—both haunted and enchanted. It was possible, I knew now, for a place to be both at once, for a person to be both at once, and as I knelt and touched the water, then placed my damp hand on my forehead, I was both the giver and the recipient of the blessing—the blesser and the blessed.

47

FEEL-GOOD, FREEWHEELING, EARTH-LOVING, ASHEVILLE-SCENTED VIBES

"I LOVE YOUR shirt!" a guy called to me at Whole Foods on Earth Day in Asheville.

Later, I bumped into him in the yogurt section.

"That really *is* a nice shirt," he said.

The first mention was nice, the second on the verge of creepy—creepy*ish*—but I took his enthusiasm in the spirit in which I believed he intended it, a spirit of celebration. And to be fair, it was an exceptionally cheerful blouse. Coral and red with swirly patterns, it was Pharrell's "Happy" in shirt form, and over two years into a pandemic, who didn't need more happy? Still, I avoided the guy, which wasn't easy since this was a relatively small store, and I had to dodge him twice more, once in the popcorn section and again in the hot-pizza area.

Finally, I made it to the checkout, where, after ringing up my order, the cashier asked whether I had Amazon Prime so I could receive the "discount." I did have Prime, but I didn't have a physical card, and I never could remember my password or PIN or whatever I was supposed to have, and anyway I had been down this road one too many times. The reward was never more than $2 no matter how many paychecks I spent, and the hassle of trying to enter the appropriate account information felt overwhelming, so I said I didn't have Prime (which was a lie, but not a big lie or a lie that affected anyone else, just a lie of expediency, and you can see the slippery slope of my ethical reasoning here, but that's not the point of this story . . .). Anyway, as luck would have it, as I said I didn't have a card, the customer behind me rifled through her purse and whipped out her card.

"Here! She can use mine."

I almost refused—again, for the sake of expediency and all—but she was so earnest, so happy to offer. I thanked her, and she passed her card to the cashier, who swiped it and announced that I had saved a total of one dollar, which caused the card's owner to apologize, but for what I wasn't sure. For offering her card in the first place? For setting us all up for disappointment?

"That's okay!" the bagger said reassuringly. "Every little bit counts."

And then we all—the lady, the cashier, the bagger, and I—agreed that you just never could tell, and it had certainly been worth trying, and who couldn't use an extra dollar these days? There was so much optimism in the air, so much communal spirit, and it did occur to me then that maybe they had sprayed some extra patchouli in the air in honor of Earth Day or that everyone except me was high, but I sensed that it was better not to question good energy, to just go with it, you know? So I thanked the woman again, told the bagger to have a really good one, and headed out to my car. *You should learn to be friendlier*, I told myself, just as a woman called to me from across the parking lot.

"I like your haircut!" she hollered.

Long-legged and glamorous in an earthy sort of way, she was draped in a lightweight blue sweater that perfectly matched her Prius.

"Thank you!" I screamed back. And before I could change my mind, I added, "I like your sweater!"

As soon as I said it, I knew it was true. Her sweater was beautiful. Her Prius was beautiful. She was beautiful. The cashier and bagger and the woman behind me in line and the stranger who had complimented my blouse were all beautiful. Maybe it was all the organic, hippie vibes or some wacky, New Age-y spell, but just for a moment, I loved everyone and everything on the planet, which didn't happen often, but there it was, here it was, gratitude creeping in, like this is how every moment is supposed to feel, like this is how every moment might feel if only I could wear this exact outfit every day for the rest of my life because part of me still believed that it was just the shirt, but for just a moment I allowed that it might be God or the gods or the goddesses or all of them combined. I didn't know for sure, since I was new to this whole gratitude thing, but I did know when to take a good long whiff of the feel-good, freewheeling, Earth-loving, Asheville-scented vibes and simply be glad.

48

COMMON

A STUDENT SAT across from me at my desk that curved like a *c*. I sat in the center, in the *c*'s belly, and she sat on the edge, the bottom. Both of us stared at our open laptops, our shared document that would become her final creative project in my outdoor-writing workshop.

"Go another beat or two here," I said. And, "Work on expanding this section. Add some reflective voice here." But mostly I just said, "This is so beautiful. This is so lovely. This is so true." And it was.

Through my cracked window, jazz strains drifted over from the music building next to us. It was spring and almost nighttime, but not quite, and the light in the room kept shifting. A shadow on the bookshelf, no, the desk, no, the carpet by the door. A large banner hung over my desk—*Abide No Hatred*—my one attempt at decoration in this office that felt so temporary, a stop along the way since, due to my lecturer status, my contract was up for renewal every couple of years.

Floor-to-ceiling bookshelves lined two walls, but my books didn't cover one full shelf. The office had formerly belonged to a department chair, then an administrator who transferred back to the department before retiring. I had moved into it during COVID to allow more space for conferencing, but it was really an office for someone up and coming, or someone who had already arrived, someone who planned to stay for the long haul, a metaphor made more insistent by the constant mechanical noise emanating from the walls and ceiling, a not-so-low hum, like a barge or a cargo ship. Maintenance crews had come to check the noise more than once. They had ripped out panels and fiddled with and adjusted things. For a day or so afterward, the noise subsided. And then it returned with renewed furor, more insistent than before.

Truthfully, I had never felt fully at home here in this office specifically, in academia more generally. The titles. The rituals. The hoops. The rigid hierarchy. It was the sort of life that could kill a creative spirit if you let it. But this job was not my life. I stayed only for the money, for the health insurance, and for moments like this. Still, as much as I loved this student and her work, the semester was almost over, and I was spent. My mind was already packing my work bag, gathering my keys, closing the office door, walking down four flights of stairs, getting in my car, driving down Merrimon Avenue, then Biltmore Avenue, then Hendersonville Road, then Airport Road, then Boylston Highway, then Asheville Highway, then, finally, to the road that led to our gravel road, the mountain hollow where I lived much as my ancestors had lived, in an old cabin in an even older holler surrounded by hills over a billion years old. *Imagine that.*

The first day of class, this student and I had talked about where I was from, about forty-five minutes south of here, and where she was from, about the same distance northwest. Place was central to everything she was writing, to everything she was. She wrote, too, about the people she loved, people I also loved, not the *exact* people, of course, but people so much of this place that I recognized them immediately in her writing, knew them as my own. I recognized something else, too, a way of looking at things, a certain way of getting to the point, all gentle and circuitous, the rhythms of speech slow and easy and familiar—*like family.* I had seen it in her the way she must have seen it in me because, as we were wrapping things up, as I reminded her of the time for our final exam and asked whether she had any questions, she closed her laptop and paused.

"I want to ask you something. I feel like I can ask you because you're Appalachian."

"Sure," I said. "You can ask me anything."

She paused again, her eyes wide and full of tears.

"I think I want to leave home and go somewhere else for a while."
She was almost whispering now. "But what if I do, and my grand-
mother gets sick or dies while I'm gone? What if everything changes?"

And, oh, oh. What did you say at a moment like that? What was
the right advice when everything always changes, not always for the
better? There was no way of knowing. You had to choose even without
knowing how it might end. And even though I heard her saying she
wanted to go other places, do other things, I saw something else or
maybe I heard it or maybe I just wanted to believe I heard it. I heard
her asking for permission or maybe just a reason to stay.

"You don't have to leave," I told her. "You don't have to leave here
to be someone."

Then again, she was asking me, a woman who, for over fifty years,
had rarely lived more than fifteen minutes from where she was born, so
for her sake, I tried to see it the other way, too, how she wanted to see
new things, do new things, become someone new. There was no shame
in leaving, either, I told her.

"Are you worried that if you stay, you'll be trapped here?" I asked.

She knew what I meant. The lack of jobs, the drugs, the poverty,
the homophobia, the sexism, the racism, the Trumpism—all the *isms*,
the hopelessness of it all. She nodded, and the tears fell freely then.
For all the years of my young adult life and into middle age, I stayed
here because I, too, wanted to be there for my grandparents when
they got old. And they did get old, and so did my parents, and so
did I, and who is to say whether or not I made the right choice? The
other life, the one I might have had, exists now in some other universe,
some other parallel time, and I am left with only this one, which has
been full and rich and beautiful but also hard at times. I have stayed
long enough to witness the destruction of our natural resources, the
rapid and unchecked development of our land, the displacement and
disillusionment of working-class Appalachian people. I have relatives,
cousins and such, who have been beaten by this place, who will never
grow old at all. All the people who loved this student, her parents and

grandparents and aunts and uncles and cousins, would tell her to stay. I saw that now. What she wanted from me was permission to grieve what she would leave behind.

"You should go," I said. "But you're right. It won't be the same when you get back. Nothing ever stays the same, and that's a hard, hard thing."

Outside in the lobby, a student tip-tapped on his keyboard. Two other students walked by talking about exams, something about papers due, and all the while the massive ship groaned and moaned, and still my student and I held each other, held our people—the ones who had left, the ones who had stayed, and the ones who had stayed and left just the same.

49

CAR DROP

WALKING ALONG THE Appalachian Trail in eastern Tennessee, five men and seven women—this will become important in a moment—navigated a rocky ledge above the Nolichucky River. Below, the river churned white—shaved ice. Just beyond the bridge, Uncle Johnny's hostel promised "good times ahead." It also promised beds (three different types, if you count a hammock as a bed, which I do not), forty-cent Snickers, and a free shuttle to the trailhead. I tried not to look over the edge too long lest I become dizzy and careen off the mountainside. Instead, I focused on the trail. The lead group, maybe four or five of the most seasoned hikers, traversed the rocks with no trouble whatsoever and stood waiting on the other side while I sat and scooted down the boulders. Not even a half mile in, I was already a spectacle.

Though I had lived my whole life in this area, I often hiked the same trails the same ways. I had recently joined this hiking group because I decided I needed to mix up my routine, to see some places I had not yet seen, to meet new people who liked to do the things I liked to do. Given that most of these hikers were fifty-plus (some of them quite a ways past fifty), I had assumed this would be more of a meander in the woods with frequent stops to observe trillium and May apples and wild iris and Jack-in-the-Pulpits. But you know what they say about assuming . . .

A few steps onto the trail I quickly realized that, despite regularly running and lifting weights and hiking, I was the lightweight of the group. The other hikers were *fast*, their hiking pace more like my running pace, and they were geared up with water-wicking everything, ultralight, breathable this and that. Without exception, they had hiking poles. *It saves your joints*, they told me. (Later, when I asked one of the women whether any of the other leaders hiked any slower, she said one woman went slightly slower, but then again, she was *ninety-four*.)

In my pack, I carried a La Croix, a turkey-mozzarella-mustard sandwich on a Hawaiian roll, and a bag of dill pickle chips from Trader Joe's. I wore the boots my dad had found abandoned at a trailhead almost a decade earlier. Back then, they had been in good condition, and they were *almost* my size, *almost* a good fit. Now the toe was separating from the shoes, and it kept catching on roots and twigs. Soon I lagged behind the others, and by the time I got to the clearing where the other hikers had gathered, the leader was already making an announcement. Well, *announcement* might be an overstatement.

"Men up!" he shouted.

And just like that, the men scurried around the next bend in the trail. Then, without preamble or explanation, the women all shuffled a few feet off the trail, dropped their pants, and squatted down. Sunlight filtered through the trees and illuminated six bare bottoms. All around me, urine poured onto dry leaves. A chorus of urine. Urine in surround sound. And then I realized that this must be trail-break protocol. Men up, women behind (so to speak).

I was not exactly the comfortable-with-my-naked-body type. At my YMCA locker room, other women strutted around completely naked—flipping at the waist to blow-dry their hair, propping their legs up on benches to apply lotion, pressing their bare bellies into the counter as they put on makeup, carrying on whole conversations with perfect strangers without one stitch on. And more power to them! Good for them! However, I was not one of those women. I was more of a pull-your-underwear-then-your-pants-on-while-still-clutching-the-towel-around-you type. And now I was going to need to pee in front of all these people.

Cursing the six cups of coffee I had had that morning, I looked desperately for a large tree to crouch behind, but there were only shrubs. I could try to wait, but what if there wasn't another stop? Plus,

I didn't want to seem rigid, like I thought there was anything whatsoever awkward about dropping my pants and peeing right in front of God and the birds and squirrels and six women I had met only a few minutes before, so I moved a few feet away from the nearest pee-er.

Then, hoping my backpack at least partially obscured my backside, I crouched on a bed of moss as nonchalantly as possible, and though I was afraid I wouldn't actually be able to pee, the way I sometimes couldn't pee if there was someone next to me in a public bathroom stall, suddenly the sound of all that free-flowing urine transformed into a bit of liquid courage, and before I knew it, there I was group-peeing in the woods, too, like the real, honest-to-God outdoorsperson I've always wanted to be, like someone who had always lived like this, like every day was some big adventure, like no one was looking over my shoulder or telling me it was too late for this or that, like there was just this day, this one day, and I had known all along that my life would be just like this trail, not an in-and-out or a loop, more like a trail where you do a car drop at the end point. One group shuttles the other to the trailhead, and you walk together from one end to the next, some of you faster, some of you slower, and then you all come out together on the other side and shuttle back to the starting point, and there you are, just like that, back at the beginning, renewed and exhausted and grateful to know, at last, this is how it is.

It all comes around in the end.

50

LIGHT UP MY LIFE

ONE NIGHT IN early May, my husband, daughter, and I stood in our driveway and peered into the woods as dozens of yellowish-greenish lights, each lasting several seconds, flickered in the darkness. One here. Another there. The sight was dizzying, disorienting. At first, the flashes appeared several feet off the ground, as if a search party were making its way through the woods, their flashlight beams aimed toward us. Soon, though, we realized that the lights only *seemed* to be high because we were standing at the foot of the steep bank. Actually, they hovered no more than a couple of feet in the air, tiny UFOs, otherworldly beacons. The sky melted into the treetops, the lights into the sky, until all around us, there was no earth and no sky, no beginning and no end, only stars. The whole scene was eerie—*ghostly.*

As soon as I thought it, I realized we were seeing blue ghost fireflies, a rare and elusive species of bioluminescent beetles visible for only a couple of weeks in May or early June each year. According to Appalachian legend, the lights are the souls of Confederate soldiers killed in these mountains, and their presence is so ethereal, so simultaneously startling and delightful, that it is possible to believe anything, except perhaps that they are bugs, which they are.

All my life, I had heard about them, but I had only seen them once before, a small cluster in a roadside ditch near where we used to live. Local companies sometimes offered guided night hikes to viewing spots in the nearby national forest and in DuPont State Forest, but due to the fireflies' fragile habitats, wildlife officials discouraged people from venturing out on their own to find them. In addition, flashlights interfered with their beetle-y communications. In the decade or so we had been living in this wooded hollow, we had never seen them here.

Each night after dinner, the three of us donned headlamps, turned the lights to red, then headed out to watch the firefly display, and each night, we were entranced, enamored anew. Below us, moonlight illuminated the pasture, reflected off the tin roof on the barn. Up the road, lights from inside our cabin spilled onto the driveway. There, the world seemed perfectly normal, business as usual. But in the dark underbrush, where rhododendrons, azaleas, wild roses, and blackberry and blueberry bushes thrived, where, if you looked closely, you could also find bloodroot, ginseng, fairy wand, rattlesnake plantain, May apples, stinging nettle, turkey brush, galax—all sorts of earthly treasures—dry and rotting leaves blanketed the forest floor, creating the ideal blue ghost habitat. The lights spilled down the mountainside, across the driveway, into the grassy pasture, then over the creek and into the forest beyond.

Blue ghosts spend the first one to two years of their lives in a larval state. They thrive in leaf debris on moist forest floors, where they feast on snails, worms, and small insects. Then, when the time is right, the males transform and take flight in search of a mate, and the limbless, wingless females remain on the ground, lighting up to show their suitors their position: *Here I am. Here I am.* There are close to fifty different species of fireflies, but even now I struggle to describe how not like "regular" lightning bugs—the lightning bugs I trapped in mason jars when I was a child—these creatures were. It was partly their size and the color of their light, but it was also the way they moved, not flying, exactly, more like drifting or floating, and if you stood in a particular spot, you were not watching them. You were part of them, surrounded by, enveloped in—no, *consumed* by—light.

Though the lights seemed to have a greenish hue, to some people, the beetles' light appears blue, hence the name, and photographers have tried and failed to capture them as they appear to human eyes. Pictures taken using long-exposure lenses give viewers a sense of how much light they emit, but the result is more like a laser show at a Trans-Siberian Orchestra concert, amped-up, psychedelic energy. It does not come close to replicating what I experienced, which was more visitation than performance, more fairy tale or dream or maybe even vision. The show was mesmerizing, meditative, soothing, like staring into a fire.

Speaking in hushed tones, as if talking aloud might break the spell, we tried different viewing locations—by the blueberry bushes, by the wild roses, near the cluster of hostas. Other than the splat of insects against the leaves as they landed, the only sounds were water running from the creek and the waterfall, the chirping of spring peepers. On the third night, we discovered the best spot to see them was farther down the driveway, just past the bridge where the road curves through a rhododendron thicket. There, hundreds of lights illuminated the hillside to our right, the bank to our left, the road in front of us and behind us and beside us. Below us, dozens of lights glowed along the creek's belly, little lascivious luminaries with—I could see it now—an eerie blue hue. All around us, the girls' suitors glistened and glowed. We were surrounded, ensconced, cradled in a conclave of fairies, a symposium of angels, carried away and caught up in an orgy of light, a cadre of cavorting lovers, a silent disco, a delicate frenzy of illicit liaisons for which perhaps the females would later give glowing reviews.

In the presence of those apparitions, lines shimmered. My vision blurred, and it was impossible to tell what was real or imagined, what was of this place and time or of another. And without being aware of remembering, with what I could later only describe as being transported, I was twelve years old again, at a Moravian love feast in the fellowship hall of the Presbyterian church where I was raised.

Held each year near Christmas, the solemn service involved traditional Moravian buns, hot apple cider, Scripture readings, hymn singing, and a ceremonial passing of light. Each participant was given a single candle, and at the designated moment, someone dimmed the overhead lights, and ushers appeared at each row to light the candle of the person on the end. That person, in turn, lit the candle of the person next to her and so on and so forth until the hall was awash with light.

Though I did not enjoy singing and was not very good at it, my best friends were members of the youth choir, so I was too. This year, perhaps in an act of generosity or perhaps because no one else would do it, the choir director had given me a brief solo in the hymn "Morning Star O Cheering Sight." Donned in black robes, my fellow choristers and I were seated on the stage just behind the speaker's podium. The soloists were all in the front row. As we began singing, we carefully tilted our lit candles, encircled with a round paper guard to protect our skin against hot, dripping wax, to light the candle of the person next to us, all while reading the music propped on stands and watching our choir director. It was a lot to ask of a group of middle schoolers, but soon the room was aglow, and for a few moments it was lovely and peaceful.

Then it was time for my solo, my moment to shine, just two lines, repeated: "Thy glad beams, thou Morning Star, cheer the nations near and far." How hard could it be? I knew the words, had practiced them for days, but just to be sure I didn't miss anything, I leaned over to get a closer look at my music, and as I did so, my long hair fell forward and grazed the candle flame. There was the softest *whoosh* and a bright flash, and for a long moment no one moved. Perhaps we all mistook it for a holy light, or perhaps we were all just focused on the task at hand. Then I smelled something acrid, pungent, and my friend Laura, sitting next to me, ripped her music sheet off the stand. She slapped me once on the head, lightly, then harder, again and again. Within seconds, the flame was extinguished, but a sizable chunk of my hair had been singed. Nonetheless, I finished my solo, the song concluded, and after a few closing words from the minister, we were done.

That night, as I stared at myself in the mirror, brushing and arranging and rearranging my hair, trying to hide the roughly four-inch-by-four-inch gap on one side, I was simultaneously despondent over my appearance and still warm from the sweet cider and flaky bread, the memory of my vocal debut, the promise of the coming Lord, and the thoughts of one of the choirboys—sweet, dark-headed, suntanned, basketball-playing, football-playing, water-skiing Sammy. Just typing all that now exhausts me, but back then I did not know myself very well, and I thought Sammy was just my type.

For the rest of December and most of January, I pulled the burnt ends of my hair back into barrettes and sprayed my mother's Jovan musk on my neck and wrists to cover the forest-fire smell that followed me everywhere. By Lent, my hair had grown back in, and Sammy and I were officially a seventh-grade item. By Pentecost, however, our romance had fizzled out. I was done with sporty boys, God-fearing boys, and my sights were set on an older, shaggy-haired stoner named Shannon. Destined to die an early death, back then Shannon was just the right level of dangerous. Every evening, I lay on the aquamarine carpet in my parents' bedroom, my socked feet pressed against the blue wall, a matching rotary phone wedged against my shoulder—*so much blue*—as he murmured in my ear.

"Say 'I love you,'" he cooed.

"I love you."

"No, no, not like that. Say it like this: '*I . . . love . . . you*.'"

Softer. Breathier. *In italics*.

Twisting the phone cord tighter around my fingers, I tried again and again to get it right, to say it right but also to do it right, to love softer and harder all at once, which is to say, to shine my light *just so*. All these years later, I am still trying, still reaching for the brightest, gentlest version of me.

After all is said and done, each female blue ghost lays up to five hundred eggs in the damp soil, five hundred promises of fireflies to come, five hundred magical beacons. How incredible is that, how simply wondrous—one worm no larger than a grain of rice lighting up our lives, giving birth to so much brilliance? And how wondrous are we, you and I, little beacons ourselves, waking up each morning full of new dreams, new possibilities, new incarnations of us?

What sort of life did I imagine for myself back in that church fellowship hall? Who did I want to be? As hard as I try to remember, I cannot. My guess is that I did not have a clear vision, that I did not look to the future and see a particular me, that I simply followed my gut, took one turn after another and another until I ended up here, not yet old but no longer young, still shining this little light of mine among a bunch of rotting leaves, saying to the man I have loved for over forty years, *Look at me glistening here by the creek. Look at this beautiful life we have lit upon.*

And to all of you, you fruitcake bakers and taco makers, you hanging-in-there trail runners and gravel-road cartwheelers, you sidewalk sitters and hot tub loungers and Prince lovers and gin-sipping pie-for-breakfast-ers, to all of you joyfully chasing down surprisement whenever and however you can, I say, softly, breathily, *in italics—I see your magical lights, all your bioluminescent goodness. Shine on, my loves.*

Shine on.

GUIDING QUESTIONS: CREATING YOUR OWN JOY DOCUMENT

Unlike with fruitcake or banana pudding or trifle, no perfect recipe for joy exists. Perhaps the process of discovering more joy in your life is less like baking and more like crafting a fine stew: toss in a bit of this, a bit of that—a pound of stew beef, a chopped onion, a couple of garlic cloves, a few diced carrots and potatoes, some salt and pepper, a little stock to keep it all from sticking—all the while remaining flexible, open, aware of nuance, alert to possibilities, open to experimentation, to adding a bit more salt or tossing in a few splashes of wine or a couple of shallots or a sprig of thyme if it needs a little something *more*. Only by using all your senses, by watching and smelling and tasting and waiting and tasting again, will you know when the stew is right.

Finding joy is a lot like that—a waiting game. A watching game. A smidgeon-of-this-and-a-sprinkling-of-that game. Still, you have to start somewhere, so below are some questions designed to help you begin your own Joy Document. Of course, this is not an exhaustive list of questions to consider, but perhaps these can serve as starting points. And who knows? You may begin with something small, a song you love, a saying you find intriguing, an awkward interaction with a man on a trail or at a produce stand or along a canal, and one joyful moment will inspire another and another until you have a whole Joy Dissertation, a Joy Treatise, a Joy Manifesto, a Joy Declaration.

Feast for a moment on that.

1. What song(s) do you associate with pivotal times in your life, and why?
2. Think about a favorite family recipe. Whom do you associate with the recipe? What events? What feelings? When do you make

this food? Have you changed the recipe at all from the original? Why or why not?

3. When in your life has a surprise risen to the level of suprisement?

4. Consider a time when an encounter with someone else caused you to think more deeply about a social/cultural/political issue that matters to you.

5. Discuss a strange/awkward/unexpected interaction with a stranger that led you to consider something in a new way.

6. In what ways have your beliefs served as a source of joy/comfort for you?

7. Point to a moment when something you once deeply believed changed irrevocably.

8. How have your interactions with animals and/or the natural world shaped what you believe?

9. Discuss a time when you learned something you didn't know you needed to learn.

10. Discuss a time when you said (literally or in spirit) "fuck it" to something, when you let go of something that was interfering with your happiness.

11. Discuss a time when you took a chance you're now glad you took.

12. What are some stories you have told yourself about your life that might not be fully true? How might revising those stories change you?

13. If you considered your body a sacred space, how might that change how you move in the world?

14. What big questions seem most pressing to you in this season of your life? What is it you most want to know?

15. In what ways might wondering (the verb—i.e., wanting to know something) lead to wonder (the noun—i.e., a sense of awe)?

ACKNOWLEDGMENTS

I have been told more than once by people who believe in strict definitions of such things that my writing is not spiritual since I don't claim any particular spiritual tradition or path. Still, I've always had a strong sense that my writing is a spiritual practice of sorts, that I belong more in a world that leaves room for mystery and wonder than one that does not. Or, put another way, my work is a place where I have tried to allow for possibilities, for the *what ifs* and *what might be*s and even for the occasional *what-might-have-beens*. So here I am, elated and grateful to have found such a welcoming home for these odd, spiraling essays, these efforts to reach for something worth saying, which is to say, for something true.

Of course, writing a book is never a solitary effort, and I am grateful to all those people who supported me in the writing and publishing of this one. First of all, I am enormously indebted to my agent, Kelly Thomas, who has so enthusiastically and, well, *joyfully* championed this work. I am also so grateful for my editor, Lisa Kloskin, who has offered much gracious and gentle wisdom along the way. Huge thanks also to Lil Copan, former Broadleaf editor, who believed in this work when it was just an idea and a few journal entries. Without Lil's support, this book simply would not be.

A couple of these essays first appeared in other places, so many thanks also to Mary Mitchell and the other editors at *Image* for first publishing "Revision" and to *Barrelhouse*, where "Subjunctive Mood" first appeared in a slightly different form. I am also immensely grateful for the friends who appear in these pages. Thanks, y'all, for allowing me to include you here but mostly for showing up in my life and teaching me again and again how to find the sweet spots.

And last but never least, my deepest gratitude goes to my husband and children, for always pointing me toward the light. You are, as always, my truest and bluest ghosts.